Other Books by Eric Krimmel

Jimland

15 Moments

Illuminate: The yearlong photo-a-day project

Uncut Garden

www.erickrimmel.com

Copyright

The Cross Country Adventures of the
Blue Highways Cycling Elite

Eric Krimmel

Acknowledgements

I wish to express my gratitude to my riding companions, Mark Poublon and Gary Oshnock for helping to refresh my memory, verify the accuracy of certain events, and their comments and criticisms.

Also, I'd like to thank Elizabeth Krimmel, Anita O'Brien and Ann Baker for their assistance in editing.

Contents

Prologue

I worked on this story for a number of years, writing in spurts then letting it sit for months, eventually turning it into a magazine article that no one wanted mainly because it was too long. After I cut out far more than I was comfortable with and turned it into something that could run as a two part story, I still didn't get any bites. A while back, I started from scratch when I realized I could turn the story into a novel and self publish, but knew it would be a big project and had to finish some other things first. So it's been quite a few years between when we finished the trip and when this book was published and there have been a couple of notable changes.

The touring maps we used are issued by the Adventure Cycling Organization and parts of the routes we rode have been changed and new routes have been added. For example, a route between Niagara Falls and Detroit is available now, that wasn't when we did our trip. This is one of the reasons I didn't specifically name restaurants and campgrounds, the other being that a business can go bankrupt over-night or the quality of service and food could instantly change with a new owner. It's possible that some of the campgrounds and restaurants we used are gone and a good chance that many have changed in one way or another. Besides, this is a story about an experience, not a guidebook.

I also didn't list prices or talk about the cost of things because everything invariably goes up, and over time, the figures become meaningless.

The biggest change however, has been the rapid advancement of technology, and specifically how common it's become to have easy access to information. Smartphone technology wasn't available when we did the trip. Not in a practical way, at least. We didn't have instant access to the internet, GPS, and maps plus the constant contact of friends, family and the rest of the world. In fact, mobile phones were just becoming common and coverage was spotty outside urban areas plus roaming fees were costly. It just didn't seem like a worthwhile item to take. Mark and I didn't carry a phone with us on the entire trip. Gary had one when he was in Canada and on the Great Lakes segment, but didn't use it much.

I can now imagine having access to maps and related information when we were off route as the major advantage of this technology. Yet, if I took the trip again there's a good chance I wouldn't take a phone. For me, a large part of the experience is breaking away from your regular life and the routines and environment that have shaped who you are and how you live. There are few experiences more exciting than a new adventure, something that is different than what you're used to. And there is nothing more that can bind you to your normal existence than a smartphone. Once you are reading the latest news story, replying to texts and email and listening to a popular song you've already heard 100 times, there is really no difference if you are doing it while sitting at your desk at work, or standing by your bike on the vast prairie of central Montana eating a granola bar while taking a break after having rode 20 miles against a strong headwind.

I can't speak for anyone else but I don't want an experience that is just like my regular life, I want something different.

And that's what I got.

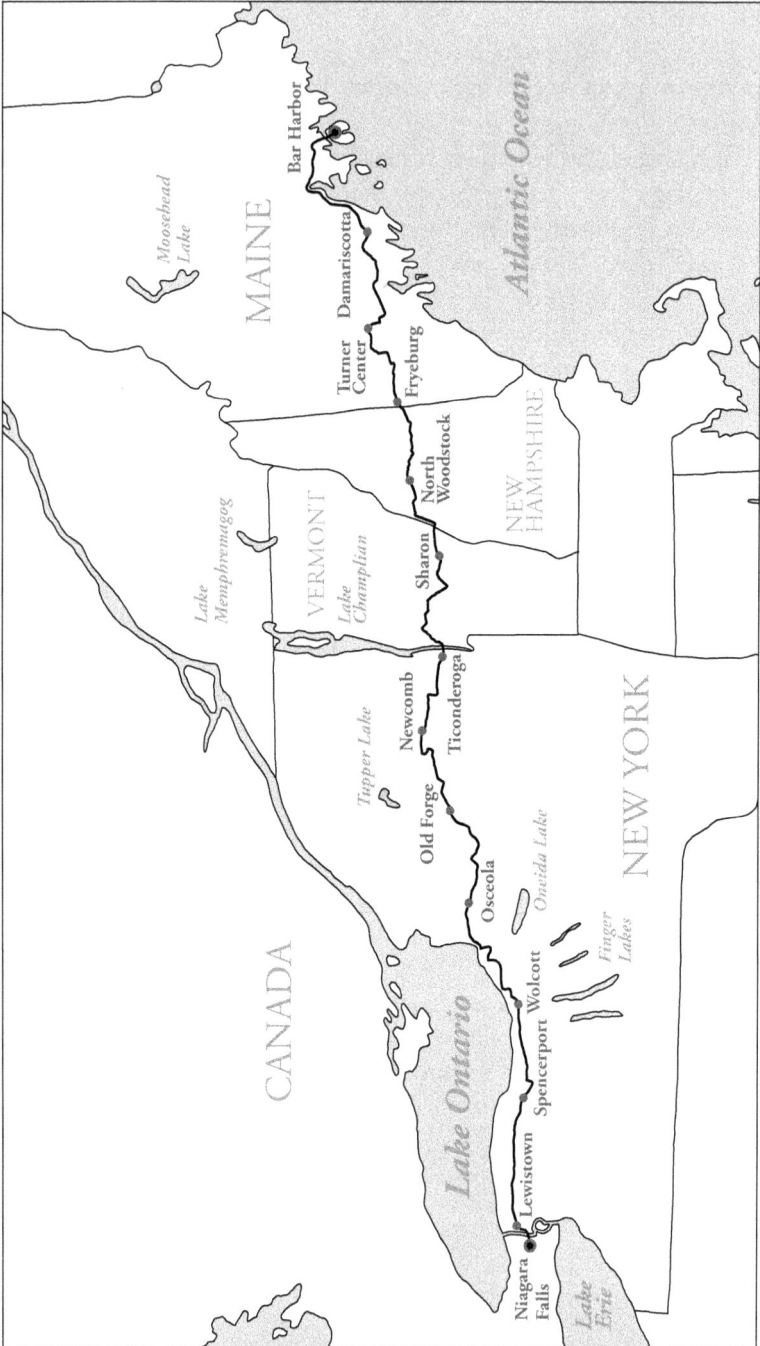

MAINE

Moosehead Lake

Bar Harbor

Turner Center   Damariscotta

Fryeburg

North Woodstock

NEW HAMPSHIRE

VERMONT

Lake Memphremagog

Lake Champlain

Sharon

Newcomb   Ticonderoga

Tupper Lake

Old Forge

Osceola

Oneida Lake

Finger Lakes

NEW YORK

CANADA

Lake Ontario

Wolcott

Spencerport

Lewistown

Niagara Falls

Lake Erie

Atlantic Ocean

8

East

Gary, Mark and I are a week into the trip on a back road in upstate New York gliding along a lightly traveled two lane highway. We're riding abreast through a thickly forested area, the sun filters through tall trees and we're casually talking when Gary says, "We need a name for our group." Mark and I start making suggestions that are similar to bike clubs and groups we're familiar with when Gary says, "No, it's got to be something like..." and now with a little reverence in his voice, "...The Elite."

Mark and I start laughing so hard we nearly lose control of our bikes. "The Elite?" Mark says, between laughs, "It would be more accurate to call us the Three Stooges of Bike Touring."

He's right. Up to that point we had made a number of mistakes and neither our fitness level nor experience as cyclists is much to brag about. To call us elite is an exaggeration of grandiose proportion. However, since the object of our group tends to be how hard we can make each other laugh, it's an entirely appropriate suggestion.

Mark and I have been friends since high school. Gary met Mark through work and all three of us have participated in both casual and organized rides together. Mark and I also rode in the Michigander three times, a week-long bike trip in which most of the route is on Rail Trails, and trucks carry your gear. None of us had done any touring, but we were ready to try some.

For over a year, Mark and I casually looked at a variety of options until Mark came across a set of maps for long distance routes in Adventure Cycling magazine. Each series of maps is a route on paved back roads and secondary highways. They give additional information like campsites and bike shops along with mileage and elevation gain and some general information about the area you're riding through. If you link a few of the series together you can ride from coast to coast. We were looking specifically at the northern cross-country route from Anacortes, Washington to Bar Harbor, Maine through our home state of Michigan.

At first, a cross-country trip seemed a bit gutsy for a couple of guys with no previous touring experience, but the 2-3 months needed to do the trip is the real obstacle. After a few discussions we were able to solve both problems by breaking the trip into 4 segments: East, Great Lakes, Plains, and West. This will allow us to take 2-3 weeks of vacation time a year, over 4 years, give us the opportunity to learn from our mistakes, fine tune our gear and technique, and allow us to modify the route slightly to pass through our hometown in the Detroit area.

Initially, as word gets around there seem to be quite a few people who are interested in the trip. When we meet in the middle of winter to talk about a specific plan, a handful show up and when we finalize the plan and start to organize the trip, three of us are committed to the adventure. We decide to start on the east coast, and that segment will take us from Bar Harbor, Maine to Metro Detroit.

The first issue we have is getting to Bar Harbor for the start of the trip. There is no direct flight, train or bus. We consider unusual ideas like renting a car or purchasing an old truck and selling it once we reach our destination but as word of mouth spread, friends of Gary volunteer to drive us there. Mike and Trisha will then continue their road trip south toward Boston to take in a number of sights they are eager to see. It's really a stroke of luck. Every option up to that point was either time consuming, cost more than we wanted to spend, or both.

The five of us leave for Bar Harbor in mid August and arrive after a two-day drive. The next morning, after breakfast, we check our maps and make our way to the start of the route. It's a warm, sunny day.

In a parking lot overlooking the Atlantic Ocean bikes are assembled, gear is loaded and adjusted and last minute photos are taken. Like little kids rushing out of school at the end of the day, we are practically giddy as we thank Mike and Trisha, wave goodbye and take off.

Our route heads directly west through a small portion of Acadia National Park but it seems foolish not to spend more time exploring the area. Without thinking about the extra miles we're adding to the day's ride, we decide on a scenic loop that will head south and take us along the coast and into the heart of the park. Acadia is gorgeous and we're glad we made the detour. The park is thickly forested but gives way to rocky shores that touch the wide-open vistas of the Atlantic Ocean. Taking in such scenery while riding under the shade of tall, hardwood trees on a warm, summer day is delightful.

Part of the joke of naming our group, The Elite, is that none of us are anything close to what could be described as a super athlete. While we had been riding, we couldn't actually call it training. Circling Acadia we experienced things we didn't foresee. The temperature was rising dramatically and the heat took its toll when accompanied by the extra weight on the bikes, and the hills. In Michigan, there's barely a 1500 ft. difference between the highest point in the state and the lowest. We're flatlanders, in the purist sense. Riding a bike uphill with a combined weight of 70 pounds or more isn't a big challenge but doing it over and over when we weren't used to it, is.

We stop a few times to take a break while watching waves crash into the rocky shore and water shoot into the air, temporarily submerge large boulders or fill inlets and swirl around in eddies. Once inland, we follow some of the many carriage roads that are closed to motorized traffic for a peaceful, secluded ride. Along the way there are numerous hills to climb and eventually we make a big loop and are back in Bar Harbor. What we thought was going to be a quick detour turned into a journey that lasted more than half the day.

We all knew that when riding uphill a cyclist's pace will slow, but now, with the extra weight on the bikes and not being used to this kind of riding, we are moving at a speed that is much slower than anticipated, covering far fewer miles than we thought in any given hour.

Because it's the height of the tourist season Mark had made reservations at campsites for our first two nights approximately 100 miles apart. In the warm, cozy den of Gary's house lounging over beers as we planned the trip, this seemed, based on previous rides and the distance we would need to cover in the time available, a fairly reasonable estimate. Mid-afternoon on the first day of the trip, reality is disrupting this fantasy and making that decision seem rather foolhardy.

Heading through town we look for street signs to pinpoint our position on the map and after some route finding we are on course. On the outside of a building I see a sign that displays the temperature and it reads, 91, and am not the least bit surprised. It is hot and humid, and combined with the roller coaster route, we are physically drained.

At the outskirts of town we follow a two lane highway that takes us into a more remote area, riding through the forest and only passing buildings occasionally. Now, as opposed to earlier when we were riding through the park, there is little shade and the sun seems merciless. It didn't feel like we got off to a great start, a number of little things combined to cast doubt on whether a trip like this was a good idea.

An hour down the road a red mini van slows and the passenger calls out, "How are you guys doing?" It's Mike and Trisha. They had spent the day sightseeing in town and around the park. "We've got some cold drinks in the cooler. Do you want some?" Yes. Oh, yes, please. There is a dry paste in my mouth that the warm water I have just can't get rid of. They pull off to the side of the road in front of us and offer sandwiches too. At this point it had been a while since we had anything substantial to eat, so we eagerly accept.

"How's it going? Mike asks.

I wipe the sweat off my forehead with my shirtsleeve, "This heat is brutal. And we're still adjusting to carrying the extra weight on the bikes." I look toward the ground. "We spent a lot more time in the park than we thought we would and we're not going to make our campsite reservation tonight, which means we've also covered less miles than we planned." I pause while remembering some other trips I'd taken and the problems that surfaced. In the beginning of a new adventure there always seems to be an adjustment period when reality confronts the careful planning you did and your vision of what the trip was going to be like is not exactly what happens. I look back at Mike and say, "But I think it's going to be okay."

A short rest and cold drink provides the clarity of mind needed to determine our new destination. There are a couple of options down the road and a few hours later we find a campground near East Orland. As we head to our campsite, Gary eyes the adjacent lake. "I'm thinking full body immersion. What do you think, guys?"

Stiff from the ride and lightheaded from the heat, Mark and I unpack, set up the tent, then stroll to the lake. A few minutes later we are splashing around and visibly feeling better as we see Gary with his towel and clean clothes head toward the showers. I call out, "Hey, what about full body immersion?" Gary just laughs and keeps walking. "Some other time."

We had enough daylight to set up, take a quick plunge and get dinner before dark. None of us were interested in cooking since there was a restaurant across the highway and down about 50 yards. When we walk back the sun has set and a minute after I lay down, I'm out.

We break camp, pack up and go back to the restaurant for breakfast. Sitting there, we talk about the possibility of making up the miles from yesterday on top of the 100 miles we had planned to ride today. Getting used to riding with the extra weight on the bikes, the hilly terrain, and the probability that it's going to be another hot day make achieving our goal seem unlikely. There is concern about getting back to Detroit within the time we had allotted but at this point it's too hard to predict what will happen over the next two weeks. During that time we know that we will physically adapt to our circumstances, but will it be enough to get back to our original plan? We decide to play it by ear and take one day at a time for a little while.

Released from the anxiety of racing to the campground where Mark had made the next reservations, we are ready to adjust our routines and expectations to the realities and conditions of the trip.

The day is hot and sunny but slightly more temperate than yesterday. Following the map isn't difficult but there are many changes in direction and it's easy to be lulled into complacency on a long stretch and miss a turn. The terrain varies from hilly to flat and we take it in stride. Small towns are separated by large forests and we pass Verona, population 100, Rockport, population 1100, and Warren population 400.

Mark rides up next to me, "How's your handlebar configuration working out?"

"Pretty good. There's some minor tweaking I want to do when I get back but so far, so good. Using the aero bar is a little odd but getting the weight completely off my wrists every now and again has been helpful. How about you? Any issues with your wrists or fingers?"

"Not too much, it depends on how long we ride each day. If I go back and forth between the lower part of the bar and the upper part, I think it helps."

The three of us each took a slightly different approach to purchasing bikes for the trip. Gary bought his bike from a small company that provided a package that included racks and bags. Mark looked for a used bike first, thinking if he couldn't find something he'd buy a new one. Luckily, he found a slightly used bike with racks at a good price. I looked at a number of bikes then purchased a hybrid with frame specifications, tires and components that were similar to the touring bikes I saw. I did this for a couple of reasons. First, it was considerably cheaper. Second, I knew I wanted to modify the handlebars and it seemed like it would be easier with the hybrid.

A common complaint among those who spend a lot of time on a bike is sore wrists, and numb or tingling fingers. I had experienced this in the past and wanted to avoid it along with another problem I have, a knot that develops between my shoulder blades. I figured the best solution for both issues would be frequently changing my riding position throughout the day. So I replaced the straight bar that came with my bike with another one that was better suited to my idea, then attached drop handlebars and a homemade aero bar. An aero bar is attached perpendicular to the handlebars and extends forward. There are pads to rest the elbows on as a biker grips the end of the bar. It's designed to give the rider a more aerodynamic position in order to increase his speed. Mine, however, is designed for comfort with thick foam and a wide stance. I call it the BarcaLounger of aero bars after a company that makes overstuffed, reclining chairs maximized for comfort.

With this configuration I have 4 different positions that I can use to vary my riding stance and avoid placing prolonged pressure on any part of my body. Also, leaning forward when using the aero bar changes the way I sit on the seat and helps with that other common problem.

We continue through sparsely populated areas and toward the end of the day settle in a campground near Waldoboro. As we unpack, our picnic table becomes cluttered with an assortment of gear. The stove is fired up and water is set to boil. Tents are staked out and take shape as poles are inserted into sleeves. Jackets are put on, sleeping bags unfurled and gear is placed in tents.

Dinner is as easy and simple as we can make it, with an eye toward minimizing clean-up. We shower and change, then discuss logistics.

Mark starts, "We covered 74 miles today and that's better, but still short to get back home on time."

"But it's farther than yesterday, and we could make up miles by putting in some long days," Gary quips.

"Yeah, but every day we fall behind that's extra mileage we have to make up on top of the miles we have to do every day."

"Well," Gary says as a smile slowly crosses his face, "maybe if you sissy, girly men stopped playing around we could turn this into a serious bike ride," then can't help himself from laughing out loud. Mark and I are laughing too and quickly try to refute Gary's good-natured kidding.

"What do you mean? I've been carrying an extra 30 pounds of steel plates just so you guys can keep up to me," I add.

"Well," Mark says, "Eric and I aren't riding Bruce Gordon Specials so we're definitely at a disadvantage," implying that Gary is riding an elitist bike, which he isn't, but it isn't a mass produced, popular brand like the kind Mark and I have either. We poke fun at each other a while longer then conclude it's still too soon to draw any conclusions about the rest of the segment.

During the night it rained and in the morning we lazily boil water and pour it over oatmeal and hot chocolate mix for breakfast. After cleaning up, we delicately fold damp tents and pack them away.

It's a bit cooler and slightly less humid than yesterday as we continue to ride through small towns like Damariscotta and Dresden separated by patches of forest along two lane highways.

The terrain remains hilly but we're adapting. There have been numerous river crossings where the road descends to the bridge, then ascends on the other side. We pedal to gain speed going downhill and hope the momentum pulls us halfway or more up the other side. As we slow, we downshift and stand on the pedals to get to the top where the road levels off.

As we ride side by side, we talk about our gear and the total weight each of us are carrying and how that affects our stamina and progress. I didn't get a chance to ride much with the kind of weight I'd be carrying before the trip so I tried hard to trim my gear to the minimum. I had done some backpacking and had hiked extensively with a small pack so I figured the lighter my load, the better. Comparatively, Mark and Gary seem to be going with the, it's-better-to-be-safe-than-sorry strategy, understandably so since this is our first tour and we weren't really sure what to expect. As such, their bikes weigh more. What surprises me, is that once the bike is rolling it isn't difficult to keep it moving on flat terrain. It's going uphill where the extra weight seems punishing.

Mark and Gary have the typical set up: two racks, front and rear, with four bags, and tent and sleeping bag strapped to the top of the rear rack. Additionally, we all have handlebar packs.

I resisted the urge to buy a front rack and bags figuring it would force me to pare my load because I'd have less space for gear. The old camera bag I'm using for a handlebar pack is larger than usual and that gives me some extra capacity and I have a large duffel that holds my tent, sleeping bag and foam pad that I strap to the top of my rear rack and I put some clothing in there. It seems like the absence of front panniers did prevent me from carrying more, but it's hard to tell by how much. And I knew I could change things for the next segment so I was willing to experiment a bit.

The weather remains warm but it's cooler than the first two days and a cloudy morning turns sunny and lasts through the evening. At the end of the day we aren't paying close attention to the road signs and get lost because we missed a turn near, ironically, Turner Center. It's a minor issue and we quickly get back on track and find a campground for the night.

As we walk the bikes to our campsite a group of small children rush over, fascinated by their appearance and ask why they look like that. We tell them we're biking across the country and this is the gear we need for that trip. "We need to carry tents and sleeping bags and cloths and stuff like that," I say. The forthright girl, exclaims, "Wooow!" and then exuberantly asks, "Are you guys on some kind of mission?"

Gary can't resist paraphrasing that old line from a popular movie. "Yes, we're on a mission from God," and the three of us chuckle.

Things are becoming easier as we adjust our routines and expectations. As part of the trial-and-error approach, one of the routines that change is our eating arrangement. Originally we were going to be self-contained, camping and cooking all our own food. Among the three of us we have a stove, fuel, pots, cups, plates, utensils and food. After a couple of meals in restaurants versus a few in camp, we decide that if restaurants are going to be plentiful along the way, it's an advantage to use them. As we confirmed in the first few days it is simply more convenient to stop for something to eat rather than cook and clean up. Also, the food at restaurants is better than our home cooked gruel and we can pare our load by carrying snack food rather than full meals. It would be even more advantageous if we could eventually ditch the stove and related paraphernalia, this would lighten our load and give us more room in our bags.

The fourth day of riding starts with a short trip to an organic farm, that houses a small public dining room for breakfast. The smell of cinnamon buns fills the air as they are pulled from the oven at the moment we walk through the door. The two women working behind the counter are friendly and welcoming. Milk and eggs had been gathered that morning and warm, hearty bread with just-made butter accompanies everything.

We feast like royalty starting with cinnamon buns and moving to thick strips of bacon, jumbo eggs over easy and inch thick toast from bread baked an hour earlier. Giving up our spartan cooking techniques and the gruel we made never seemed like a better idea. It's cool and dreary outside but warm and comforting inside.

I am reminded of a regional expression when I ask where the bathroom is, which is small and wedged under a staircase. The woman behind the counter points and says, "It's ova tha-a. Such that it is."

We really don't want to leave, especially since it's gotten darker during our stay. When we can't procrastinate any longer, we walk out the door as rain lightly starts to fall. Another group of bikers are just pulling up. There are 10 of them and every day one couple drives the truck they've rented to transport the bikes and work as a support vehicle as the group makes it's way back to New York. Today would be a good day to drive.

We pull out the rain gear from our bags. Mark's is a bright green, a logical, reasonable choice for high visibility but he takes a little ribbing as Gary and I make references to the Jolly Green Giant. We take off and the rain picks up.

It's steady, but often tapers to a drizzle. We ride through South Paris, and Norway under dreary skies. There is a repetitive whoosh as cars pass and a persistent thud/splash as tires hit puddles. Looking for a respite from the rain and a warm place to eat we see a small diner and stop for lunch.

I follow Gary inside and the staunch of stale cigarette smoke attacks my nose. The decor is shabby and run down. It looks like a lone patron is sitting at a short bar on a stool with his back to us and there is a woman on the other side. It seems odd that there aren't more customers and Gary asks, "Are you open?"

The woman behind the bar snaps back, "This isn't Madison Avenue!"

Gary turns around and sits at the nearest table with a look on his face that says, 'What in the hell did that mean?' I only half shrug my shoulders to hide the expression from the waitress as she comes out from around the bar and hands us menus. Mark joins us and we order sandwiches and coffee. The waitress is an elderly woman of an age that you'd expect to be retired and walks with a limp to the extent that it's almost embarrassing that she is waiting on us, young able-bodied men.

The sandwiches are cold cuts and processed cheese on white bread and the coffee tastes as if had been made the previous day and was warmed up in a pan, which if it was, would not be hard to believe.

On the heels of a wonderful feast that morning is a meal at the opposite end of the spectrum. Contrary to popular belief, not all diners offer a cozy environment and first-rate food, and this is one of the worst.

Outside and unsatisfied, I notice Gary looking for his tool kit. Down the road I see a billboard for a Dunkin' Donuts a mile away and tell the guys that I'm going to go ahead for a decent cup of coffee while Gary adjusts his bike. I take off and about a half mile later see a McDonald's, figure that will work and grab a chocolate chip cookie too. I go outside and next to my bike, under the eave, stand out of the rain with a full view of the street. 15 minutes must have elapsed and I'm wondering what kind of problems the guys are having when I see Mark ride by in the opposite direction.

"HEY! MARK!" Mark's head turns toward me, then he rides up.

"Are you guys still having problems with Gary's bike?" I blurt out.

"What are you doing here?" Mark asks.

"Why were you riding that way?" I say as I motion to the right with my thumb.

"Because we were at Dunkin' Donuts looking for you."

"What? How's Gary's bike?"

"It's fine, he just wanted to adjust the rear brake. It only took a minute, we were right behind you."

Ugh. I had made a big mistake. It wasn't illogical to think that I wouldn't have missed them if they rode by but they must have done so during the minute and a half that I was inside. I said I was going to Dunkin' Donuts and I should have gone there.

We start riding and I'm pleading my case, "It wasn't crowded, I walked in, got the coffee and walked out. I must have just missed you."

"But this isn't where you said you'd be," Mark countered.

"Yeah."

We take off in a light rain to meet up with Gary. He is just down the road a bit.

"Hey, where have you been?" Gary says, laughing. He knows I messed up and doesn't want to pass up a chance to poke fun.

"Hiding from you!" I retort and we both laugh.

Gary starts pedaling as Mark and I pass and rides up next to me.

"What happened?" he says in a more serious tone.

"Oh," I quickly do a recap, "I saw a McDonald's, looked down the road and didn't see the Dunkin' Donuts and thought it might be off route, so I stopped. I figured you guys would be a while so I had enough time to duck in, get some coffee and I'd catch you riding by. Mark said you guys left shortly after I did so I was probably inside when you passed me."

"I just tweaked my rear brake, it only took a second."

"Yeah, I thought you were going to be longer." I pause for a second. "Besides, I really needed a decent cup of coffee, it's not like we had lunch on Madison Avenue!"

We both laugh as Gary pulls forward and we ride single file making our way out of town in the rain.

The rest of the day is cool and wet. We are damp and chilled and not looking forward to sorting through gear and setting up the tents when everything is soaked. Near Fryeburg we have a discussion about finding a room for the night. We come across a row of tiny cottages made to look like log cabins by rounded boards nailed horizontally to the sides, and one is available. It's nice to get out of the rain, take a hot shower and sleep in a soft bed.

Shortly after we leave the next morning we cross the state line and stop to take our picture with the, Welcome To New Hampshire, sign. It's a silly, tourist thing to do but signifies the completion of a step toward attaining our goal and we feel good about that.

We ride under sunny blue skies and high wispy clouds for about an hour before we come to Conway then head off route to North Conway. Gary had been experiencing some issues with the bottom bracket of his bike– the axle and set of bearings that the sprocket and pedals are attached to, and according to our map there are two bike shops in this small town of 2032. We are heading toward a long climb and limited services for the next 40 miles so Gary wants to have his bike looked at. Mark and I stay behind at a small park and spread out our wet gear from the previous day. Anxious to be riding, Mark and I pace around a bit then I get out my paper and pen and scribble some notes about the trip and Mark writes a few postcards. After that we try to relax in the sun but can't escape the idea that we're burning up daylight.

Eventually Gary rides up with a cardboard box under his arm.

"What took so long?" Mark asks.

Gary is surprised, "It wasn't that long, was it?"

"What's the box for?" I inquire.

"I've got to dump some of this stuff. I'm going to mail it back home. If you guys want to throw some things in here, go ahead."

After almost a week on the road, adjusting our routines and expectations, and having ridden in various conditions over diverse terrain, if anything, there are a few items I'd add the next time. But I'm not surprised Gary wants to shed some gear and he happily tosses a bunch of things into the box and Mark throws a few things in too.

"What was wrong with the bottom bracket?" Mark asks.

"I'm not sure and the guy at the shop didn't know either so I just had him replace it instead of taking time to tear it apart. While he was doing that I mailed some postcards, found this box and got something to eat."

"Oh, you already ate?" Mark says. This seems like another instance of either miscommunication or poor planning.

"Well, the guy said it was going to take 20 minutes or so. The restaurant is nearby and so is the post office. It's just down the road. If I go mail this you and Eric can eat, then we can take off."

It seemed like there were various times when one of us was holding the group up, and in our own way we all took a turn at this. By itself this is not an issue, but there is an overriding sense that we aren't covering the miles we need to each day, so any delay became a potential irritant.

Soon we are on the Kancamagus Highway as we head into and over the White Mountains. This is going to be a long uphill stretch and the map states, "NO SERVICES EXCEPT CAMPING NEXT 32 MILES." Clouds had moved in and it's a hazy afternoon, which is good because we'll be heavily exerting ourselves for the next couple of hours. At the edge of the road on the other side of the white line we only have about a foot of pavement before a drop to a wide gravel shoulder. Riding on gravel as we make our way uphill is out of the question. We hug the side of the road and proceed at a slow pace taking a number of breaks. We plod along as we exert ourselves with each stroke of the pedal.

While not as long or high as many mountain roads out west, in places the grade seems unusually harsh and we find ourselves moving at a snail's pace even in first gear. Moreover, there are a couple of places where we aren't just moving slowly, we are also pedaling so slow it's hard to maintain our balance. At one point I think it would be easier to walk the bike uphill. It isn't, and after barely 20 feet I jump back on.

Mark had bought an extra small chain ring for his bike specifically designed for this kind of situation. We teased him about it, both Gary and I, implying that we were tough enough for those uphill ascents without any extra help or equipment. Now it was Mark who was getting the last laugh when Gary also jumped off his bike and walked it for a few steps, as Mark was able to maintain enough revolutions to sustain his balance and keep moving forward.

Gary had nicknamed Mark, Blue, at the start of the trip. Now he added to that the term, Code Blue meaning to downshift into the lowest gear and prepare for a struggle. From then on, when approaching steep upgrades Gary would often shout, "Code Blue!" like a battle cry indicating we should down shift and dig in.

The pass tops out at 2855 feet and after a short rest we start down. The road initially twists around like an odd shaped keyhole and then folds into a couple of large, hairpin turns but eventually straightens into gentle curves. We make up some time on the quick descent and continue riding east until we make our way into North Woodstock. We find a restaurant, order and discuss our progress.

The uphill miles and the delay around lunchtime amounted to our shortest day yet, just 50 miles. This brought back the argument for pushing forward and riding at night. Gary had suggested on more than one occasion that we continue riding into the night regardless of accommodations in order to make up miles. We had figured we wouldn't make it back to the Detroit area by our deadline, so now it's just a matter of seeing how far we can go in order to have the shortest distance to make up.

Since studies of riding at night have shown it to be much more dangerous than riding in daylight, I'm against it. Besides, reading road signs, finding a campsite and having to set up tents and sort through gear with flashlights is a hassle. I feel we can cover more miles if we just get up earlier and don't make as many stops. This argument turns out to be a bigger issue than imagined. I routinely feel my point isn't being taken seriously and it's irritating that the mileage issue always seems to come up in the evening, just a few hours before dark, when other options are unavailable.

By the time we finish eating it's dusk and we decide to stay at a nearby campground.

The next day we find a restaurant with a patio and under the shade of a big umbrella at an outdoor table all three of us order the Hungry Man Special: two eggs, bacon, sausage, pancakes, hash browns, and toast. It's a great morning. The sun is shining, there is a slight warm breeze that chases away the cool air and we are all in a good mood, laughing and talking.

Since the previous day had been the shortest mileage day so far and the day before that, when it rained for so long wasn't much better, we are hoping to redeem ourselves today.

Mark slowly takes off while I straddle my bike and Gary zips up his pannier. "Ready?" I say, looking at Gary.

"Yeah. Oo! Just a second." We both start laughing as Gary reaches up with his left hand and lightly adjusts a small, one inch mirror that hangs just inches from his face off his helmet. It's so small it doesn't look like it would be very effective but he says it offers a good view of approaching cars from behind. The problem is that if it gets twisted even a small amount in any direction it's out of alignment and then he's looking at the sky or down at the road, or back at his own eyeball. And it gets twisted about 20 times a day. At first it seemed like a minor nuisance until it happened so often, the mere act of Gary expressing his frustration and reaching up to adjust the mirror is cause for laughter.

From North Woodstock we get back on Highway 112 and ride toward the Vermont border. We're still on a more heavily traveled road, at least more traveled than what we've been used to, but the shoulder is good and we glide along without issue. About 5 miles out we cross the Appalachian Trail, a hiking trail that stretches 2184 miles from Maine to Georgia. I feel a sense of simpatico with the hikers who are just starting out, adjusting to life on the trail and the long journey ahead of them. Like us, they most likely have the same worries and concerns but also that sense of wonder and excitement.

Eventually we branch off and veer onto less traveled roads near North Haverhill. We're on a southerly route that parallels the Connecticut River.

The riding is definitely easier a week into the trip, not because the terrain has gotten easier but because we're adapting to it. There are still short, sharp hills but now that we are more used to them we're not dead tired at the top and the thrill-inducing downhill runs on the backside are more enjoyable. As we wind along the river on these secondary highways, the curves are tighter and there are long gradual rises and leisurely gliding.

We spend about two hours heading south before we cross over the river into Vermont near East Thetford. We stop to pose for another photo in front of the, Welcome To Vermont, sign and stay for an extended rest. There is a campsite just off route but it's still early in the day and if we stop, it will be the shortest mileage day so far, even shorter than the two previous. This only comes up because it doesn't look like there's a campground for over 50 miles and there's no way we can make it before dark. Gary wants to press on and neither Mark nor I can blame him. We can always hike into the forest and pitch our tents but none of us want to do that. We have no idea what kind of accommodations are ahead but it doesn't make much sense to stop for the night now. We push on.

A few more hours down the road, as dusk settles in, we pay close attention to signs in hope of finding a cabin, bed and breakfast or new campsite that didn't make it onto the map. We're on the edge of darkness and it doesn't look good for finding a place to stay, but we ride into Sharon and discover a small motel. During the tourist season there's a good chance they won't have a vacancy but Gary goes inside and to see if they have a room available. Luckily, they do. I was thinking we'd be spending the night on the side of the road, but Gary was more optimistic believing we would find some kind of accommodations, or perhaps just putting on a good act.

"See, I knew we'd find something," Gary says as he laughs.

"Yeah, yeah," I reply, knowing he was far from sure.

We're outside grabbing our bags when a car pulls up. The motel proprietor is outside also and we're asking if our bikes will be okay if we leave them just outside the door overnight. A man steps out of the car and the manager walks over to greet him. We overhear their conversation.

"Hi, can I help you."

"Yes, do you have a vacancy for tonight."

"No, I'm sorry I just rented the last room."

Gary starts giggling. "Oh, man! You are so lucky," I quietly exclaim with a big smile on my face.

Spending the night in the forest wouldn't have been so bad but after a long day on the road it's nice to take a shower. When we were planning the trip, it seemed like there were enough campsites along the route to accommodate us. The tricky part, we realized, was finding one at the moment we wanted to camp.

Over breakfast we look ahead on the map and think we can make it into New York today. There is a campsite just outside of Ticonderoga on the other side of Lake Champlain. The mileage is good, but a bit on the aggressive side based on how far we've been riding every day and considering we'll be crossing the Green Mountains.

Once we're under way, the map points out notable features to the left and right: Blueberry Mountain, Mount Moosalamoo, Delectable Mountain, and Broad Brook Mountain. If it's possible to see these landmarks through openings in the thick forest, it would still be hard to know the exact moment to look without the guidance of a roadside sign. I'm not sure I saw any of them.

We're still crossing a lot rivers, accelerating on the downhill section toward the bridge, quickly traversing it, then rapidly downshifting as gravity pulls us part way up the other side while decelerating abruptly. Then it's a hard push on the pedals as our pace slows until we hit the top and the road levels off. Sometimes a series of hills will be spaced so that the momentum will carry you up the next one and the climbing is easier when that happens, but most of the time the terrain isn't that consistent.

So far, midday is always hot but not as bad as the first day. Mornings are cool and we ride with light jackets but the bulk of the day is mostly pleasant. Recently we've been having good luck with the weather and haven't seen rain in a few days.

Making our way along the twisting secondary highways through the Green Mountains requires a lot of taxing uphill road work. Getting over the mountains doesn't start at the lowest point and go directly uphill to the highest point. There are many short uphill challenges in which the grade sometimes varies. Since the Kancamagus Pass we had experienced a number of uphill runs that had grades that were tortuous, often encouraging Gary to shout out, "Code Blue!"

On some of the steepest hills, if traffic is light, I learned to ride across the road at a 45 degree angle then back again working my way uphill in a zigzag manner. This makes the climb a little easier but means I'm covering a greater distance so I don't use this technique unless I have to.

It's late afternoon when we stop at a convenience store to pick up some snacks and a cold drink. Suddenly I wonder what time the ferry at Lake Champlain stops operating and if it's possible we might get stranded on this side of the lake. After a brief discussion we decide to step up our pace as we race toward the New York border. The ferry doesn't stay open very late and though we arrive at dusk, we have plenty of time to make the crossing. On a boat that can carry perhaps 18 or more vehicles, a lone pickup and the three of us glide across the calm water.

Welcome To New York. Click.

It's about a two mile ride from the shore into Ticonderoga where we find a place to eat. It's been a strenuous day, first coming over the Green Mountains then a fast paced sprint to the ferry, and we're exhausted. We crossed the lake under a hazy sky and halfway through dinner clouds move in and it starts to rain. It's already dark when we finish so we hang out for a while hoping the rain will stop, but we're anxious to call it a night so we put on the rain gear and take off.

The campsite is four miles off route and we still have to find the street that will lead us there, and according to the map it looks like that could be another mile down the road. It's rarely so dark your eyes can't adjust and make out shapes but on a country road without streetlights, or headlights on our bikes, it means that we can't see street signs very well. Or potholes, glass and other obstructions on the road, either. The rain lets up and almost an hour later we find the campground, make it to our site, then fumble with gear using flashlights. Gary sees a washing machine and is going to do laundry and I could do some too. But after I clean up, I lay on my sleeping bag as Mark heads to the showers and instantly I'm out. When Mark comes back to the tent I wake, pull the sleeping bag around me and fall into a coma until morning.

The next day none of us are eager to jump up and get going. I don't look at the clock on my electronic speedometer, the only timepiece I have, but we don't get an early start. Once we're back on route we stop at the first restaurant we see. It turns out yesterday was our highest mileage day so far and in spite of riding through the Green Mountains we still covered 80 miles. Either tired from the day before, basking in our accomplishment, laziness or a combination of all, we waste away the morning. A late breakfast leads to numerous refills of coffee with no hint from any of us we're eager to ride.

I start talking about what a hassle it is to bike after dark. After our experience last night, I think it will be easy to come to a consensus that this should be avoided. I'm wrong.

"It took us a lot longer to find the campsite, we could have rolled over glass just because we couldn't see it, setting up the tents and finding gear was unnecessarily frustrating, and we almost missed the turn because we couldn't see the sign. Imagine the further delays if we had to fix a flat in the dark. All this, on top of the fact that it's just more dangerous. It's an unnecessary risk."

Gary is pushing back, "We really couldn't avoid it last night."

"That's not entirely true," I say, not wanting him to miss my point. "If we had gotten up earlier, we could have arrived in Ticonderoga two hours earlier, had dinner, got to the campsite and been set up before it rained too."

At that point Mark jumps in, "But we're on vacation and I have to get up early all year long so I'm not eager to do it now."

"I agree, I don't think any of us want to be locked into a schedule or get up at the crack of dawn."

"But we can't really avoid riding after dark, sometimes it's going to happen," Gary interjects.

"Again, not entirely true," I counter. "There are three options: disregard the mileage requirement and be satisfied with the distance we cover every day no matter what it is, develop a more rigid schedule so we cover more miles earlier in the day, or ride until we make our minimum mileage requirement which most likely means we'll frequently ride after dark based on how the trip has gone so far."

"But you just can't rule out that there are going to be times when we have to ride at night," Gary says. "Besides, if we have to be back on a certain day then we have to make sure we are covering so many miles a day. We can't ride 500 miles on the last day."

"I don't disagree with that, but if we set out with the idea that it doesn't matter if we ride at night then we'll be doing it every day because the only time the mileage issue comes up is two hours before dark, and the only option then is to ride after dark." I pause for a second then continue, "I don't want to be locked into a schedule any more than you guys do, but as a safety issue I don't want to ride at night and there are ways to prevent it and still cover the miles we need to."

Another aspect of this issue is the flexibility of our daily lives. I would have preferred to take as much time as we needed and simply enjoy the ride however it turned out. Mark and Gary aren't as flexible with their schedules and are anxious to get back so they can have a day or two off before heading back to work. I don't think anyone wants to race across the country but in spite of our planning and discussions, I'm beginning to realize each of us came to this adventure with a slightly different set of expectations.

Of the three of us, Mark is the least vocal and it's hard to tell what he is thinking. Gary leans back and sighs. It appears he is simply disregarding my argument and digging his heels in. It feels like this issue isn't going to be resolved.

We change the subject and enjoy a leisurely morning. No one wants to be the taskmaster, checking the time, restricting our breaks or implementing an inflexible schedule. And this is a prefect example of us frittering away time that could have be spent riding. The thing is, I didn't care how many miles we covered that day, Gary, and to a slightly lesser degree, Mark, did.

We get back on the road and are heading into a remote area. This is the gateway for the Adirondack Mountains and the route will take us through the heart of it for the next couple of days. Over the next few hours we seem to have left civilization behind. Traditional northwoods cabins line small lakes ringed in dense forest. Sunlight filters down through the thick canopy of trees in small patches. The distinct voices of songbirds can be heard over the quite hush. Facilities are spaced farther apart and traffic is light. We spend quite a bit of time riding side by side and casually talking and joking.

All of a sudden I hear a metal twang and there's a disturbing wobble in my rear tire. A spoke snapped and I come to a fairly abrupt stop because it pulls the wheel so out of round it's heavily rubbing the left brake pad. There is a clearing not far ahead where we can work on the bike and I disconnect the brake so I can ride up to it. I've never had an issue with a spoke, so after many years and thousands of miles of riding this comes as a surprise. I park my bike, and while I don't have a spare or a spoke wrench, I do have a small crescent wrench and plan to remove the broken spoke, then adjust the tension on the other ones to straighten out the rim as best I can. This will hold until we can find a bike shop. It won't be pretty, but I figure I can ride like that until I can get it fixed. I dig into my panniers looking for my tools and Mark and Gary do the same. I find them, look up and see Gary holding four or five spokes.

"You have spokes?" I ask. It seems like such an odd thing to be carrying because I have never had something like this happen, and yet in the next second realize it isn't so odd after all.

"Don't you?" Gary says, setting me up.

"Um…" I really didn't want to say, I don't. "No?"

"See, I *am* carrying all the community gear!" Gary exclaims as Mark and I laugh. This had become a familiar harangue. We're using Gary's stove, fuel bottle and pots and there is some other gear we split between us. We all don't need to carry an air pump for example. And we don't need to double up on tools but each of us have a slightly different idea about what to carry so there is some redundancy. Gary feels he is carrying most of the gear all of us will use. Mark and I disagree.

"Do you have spokes Mark?" Gary asks in a jokingly confrontational way.

"Yes I do. Plenty of spokes. More than enough spokes. Did you need some spokes? Because I got ya covered."

The three of us are laughing pretty hard as we begin to tear my wheel apart. The spoke is attached to the side of the hub with the cog set and a special socket is needed to remove it. That socket is something that is so rarely needed, none of us have one. We bend over the half of the spoke attached to the hub and twist it around to make a loop. Then we put a new spoke on the rim, feed the end through the loop and bent it upward to make a loop in that piece. Next we need to tighten the nut that attaches the spoke to the rim to see if our idea will work, and tighten or loosen the other spokes to straighten the rim. I grab my crescent wrench to adjust the small nuts on the end of the spokes.

"You don't have a spoke wrench either?" Gary asks.

I bow my head, close my eyes, and mumble, "Oh, my god."

Mark and Gary burst out laughing.

"You're pretty lucky I'm around and carrying all the community gear, Krimmel. If you want, you can take your panniers and strap them on top of my rack. I wouldn't mind carrying that stuff too, since I'm practically carrying everything else."

"Are we almost done, because I really think I need to ride. I need to put some distance between me and this harassment." I jokingly remark.

It's hard to true the wheel and there is still some wobble but it's bearable. Mark checks the map and it looks like we'll pass a bike shop tomorrow.

Back on the road, the traffic is still light enough that we spend quite a bit of time riding abreast and talking. We ride at a leisurely pace, in fact the whole day was rather laid back, and it ends short on mileage.

As twilight sets in, we unload gear and set up tents at a state campground. We have a secluded site at the edge of a small lake that makes it seem like we are the only ones in the park. As it slowly gets dark, the quiet is undisturbed by man-made sounds while crickets, bullfrogs and occasionally the cry of a loon, dominate the velvety night.

I'm up early. The sun is shining, though low on the horizon and our heavily shaded campsite is still chilly and covered with dew. I can't go back to sleep so I put on a jacket and get up. Everything is still, and the only sound comes from quietly chirping birds. Mist rises above the surface of the lake and I grab my camera and take some photos. I fire up the stove, heat some water and get out a packet of hot chocolate mix. I'm thinking this would be a good day to get an early start and hope the guys will hear me stirring and get up, but they seem dead to the world. It's a nice morning, calm and quiet, and cool with a nip of fall in the air.

Suddenly I remember I need to do laundry. The other night when Gary and Mark did some I was too tired. I figure it would be a good idea to ride into the next town and get it done, ideally meeting up with the guys just as I finish so none of us will be waiting around. I start packing up and when I'm ready to ride Mark and Gary are up too. They aren't too keen on my idea, perhaps based on when we missed each other last week. But I also feel if I don't go we'll be lulled into the same slow start that we usually get and then we'll be arguing again at the end of the day as to whether we should keep riding into the night, and that debate is becoming tedious. There are two towns up the road and one of them has to have a Laundromat. I'll wait for them there.

In the town of Long Lake I put my clothes in and consider finding a place to eat, but resist the urge. I go outside to sit in the sun and a woman who is also doing laundry comes out and asks where I'm heading. We talk about the trip until our cloths are ready for a dryer and almost on cue Mark and Gary arrive as I'm finishing up.

"Did you guys eat?"

"Yeah."

"I have to grab something. There's a restaurant over there," I say pointing. "It'll only take a second."

I walk into the nearly empty restaurant, order, eat and am jumping back on my bike in 15 minutes. I see Mark and Gary at the gas station across the street. Mark is putting air in his tires. I ride up, "Everything alright?"

"Yeah, I was just a little low."

We turn onto a busier road and traffic is slightly heavier even though we are still in the sparsely populated Adirondacks. The sun is bright in a barely cloudy sky but the air has a cool edge to it. My rear wheel is still out of round and I can feel the wobble as I ride, but there is a bike shop in Inlet, which is just up the road a bit.

We pass Blue Mountain Lake, both the lake and the town, which have the exact same name, and are in close proximity to Blue Mountain. After that, we are on a long stretch where we ride past what seems like a continuous series of lakes and rivers without a town in sight. Mid afternoon we come into Inlet and find the bike shop. The mechanic is working on another bike and says it will be a minute before he can get to my wheel. With the right tool the sprockets come off, then the chain guard and finally the remnant of the old spoke. The tire is deflated and pulled off and a new spoke is put in place. The rim is put on the truing stand and the mechanic spins the wheel as he tightens or loosens a variety of spokes until the rim is straight.

I find Mark and Gary lying on a patch of grass and they are eager to take off. We continue down Route 28, which parallels Fulton Chain Lakes, long thin lakes that twist back and forth and connect to Moose River. Near Thendara we find a campground, satisfied with the 72 miles we covered that day.

I feel a sense of vindication. In spite of doing laundry and stopping at the bike shop, with an early start we covered more miles than our average and found a campsite before dark. But there is no way I want to bring this up and start that argument again.

We spend most of the morning riding in a southeast direction and leave the massive Adirondack Park. Just after noon we miss a turn and by the time we realize it, stop and debate over whether we should backtrack or go forward and try to veer back on route. We are at an intersection when a truck pulls up and looks for traffic before turning. We flag him down. I have never been good with audible directions, I'm a visual guy. Give me a map, and if it's accurate I can find anything. So when the truck driver starts saying turn here and go past this and veer left and find a street with this name then go right, it makes about as much sense as if he had said, "Just click your heels three times and say, There's no place like home." Gary and Mark seem to be following him better, so we take off but after fifteen minutes of riding we stop, still not exactly sure where we are and I have no idea if we're even heading in the right direction. I argue in favor of backtracking to find the route while Gary is sure that we'll run into it a little further up. We both turn to Mark as the tie breaker. Mark pauses for a moment then says, "I think we should keep going forward." About 10 minutes later we are back on route.

We are riding into the most heavily populated area we had come across in the last few days, on a road with two double lanes divided by a grassy median with wide and smooth paved shoulders. Gary and Mark are out front riding abreast and I'm about 70 feet behind them. My neck is stiff so I bend my head down as far as it will go to stretch the muscles. Then, while I'm still riding along and looking at the ground, I bend it to the left, then to the right. In the next second I jerk forward, am flying through the air, spinning around and unable to focus on anything.

At almost the exact moment I took my eyes off the road, Gary and Mark stopped to look at the map and I crashed into the back of them. Mark's bike took the brunt of the hit and was able to absorb most of it, while Mark stood straddling it. I, however, did my best Superman imitation, hit the ground hard and slid.

Yes, I am one of the proud, the few, The Elite. What a doofus!

Besides considerable road rash, there is a steady flow of blood from my knee. Almost immediately, a worker from the nursing home across the street, who was watching us ride by and witnessed the accident, grabbed some gauze and antiseptic and ran over to us. The antiseptic didn't stop the flow of blood and I put pressure on the gauze to try and contain it. A minute later a pick-up stops to see if we are okay and offers a ride to a nearby clinic, which everyone accepts for me.

Feeling rather stupid, I try to wave off their concern but realize it would be more foolish to turn my back on these good Samaritans and the advice of my friends.

The clinic is only a few miles away and the driver calls ahead so when we get there, he grabs my bike out of the bed, I thank him and hobble inside where they are waiting for me.

I sit on the table and while I am sore, I'm not in a lot of pain. I tell the doctor that we are on a cross-country bike trip and I intend to continue the ride as he prepares to stitch my knee. I'm slashed just above the kneecap and the incision is mainly vertical which means that bending my knee thousands of times over the next couple of days shouldn't rip the stitches out or be a serious detriment to healing.

As the doctor gathers his instruments and prepares the Novocain, I try to relieve some of the seriousness of the situation. "I don't have insurance so I would like you to use the economy thread." The doctor is focused on his work but smiles and says, "Oh no, sir, only the best for our patients."

After a few minutes, he has me bend my knee a couple of times, adjusts his work, and warns me of the dangers of infection. The nurse then says the tetanus shot she is going to give me might make my arm sore and asks if I have a preference. I envision the worst case, riding along with one of my arms in a sling and I figure I could still make some progress if I can shift the gears on the rear wheel, as opposed to the three main ones next to the pedals. The gears on the wheel are controlled by the shifter on the right side of the handlebars. "Put it in my left arm."

The nurse cleans up some of the road rash and before I leave she tells me in a hushed voice that the doctor gave me a little break on the price. I thank her and go collect my bill from the front desk.

I hobble outside and Mark and Gary are working on my bike, fixing the damage as best they can. The front wheel is out of round and it doesn't look like any amount of spoke adjustment is going to make it true again, but it's not so bad I can't ride with it. There is a solemn feeling in the air as we contemplate the harsh reality that anything can go wrong at any time and will mostly likely come when you least expect it. This time, most of the damage is to my pride and ego, I'm still able to ride and the pain is tolerable. But this is the very fear that grips you before a new adventure starts, when you envision the worst of things happening.

When we're done working on the bike we look around for a place to eat. There is a pizzeria nearby and next to it a Laundromat, so we eat while Mark and Gary wash some clothes.

Back on the road, the pain in my knee is mild. I'm more concerned about the constant flexing of the joint and if it might damage the stitches and create a bigger mess than what I had. The muscles of my arm feel fine for now and the only bothersome thing is the burning sensation of road rash on my arms and legs.

Getting lost, the accident, and our extended lunch break ate up a lot of time and once again we're arguing near dusk over whether we should camp at a nearby site or ride into the dark for the next one. Not surprisingly I vote to camp, and Gary votes to ride. Mark ends up siding with me.

The campground isn't near a town or any place to eat and the guy who runs it says we can camp, "Anywhere over there," as he points to a big area with widely spaced apple trees.

The tents are set up, and gear pulled off our bikes. I start digging through my panniers for some snacks. It's slim pickings. I find some miniature chocolate bars that came from a larger bag that I had mostly devoured already and a couple of granola bars. I need to do a better job of remembering to check my supply when we stop at a store.

Before I head to the shower I find a clean plastic bag and cut it along the seams so it lays flat. I have a small amount of duct tape and use that to attach the plastic to my leg over my wounded knee, I'm supposed to keep it dry for a few days.

Later I grimace as I rip the duct tape off of my hairy thigh. I lift the edge of the bandage to find the stitches intact and everything looking as well as can be expected.

The next morning, as we start breaking camp, Gary excitedly tells us about something unusual that happened as the sun was coming up. He was awakened by the loud snort of a deer just outside his tent. Gary theorizes the deer was probably after some of the many apples on the ground. As his story unfolds, however, there seems to be a more plausible and humorous explanation.

First, Gary isn't a quiet sleeper. In fact, his snoring is loud enough that other groups he's camped with have asked him to set up his tent a little distance from theirs. A deer wandering into our camp to eat apples from the ground is feasible, however a deer walking up to Gary's tent, moving to within inches of his head and snorting so loud that Gary woke from a deep sleep seems as likely as finding a leprechaun, all things considered.

As Gary tells his story, Mark and I start smiling then laugh as Gary mentally hangs on to his snorting deer theory. He stops and looks at us quizzically. "What?" Then all of a sudden it dawns on him, "It wasn't.... My snoring?" Then all three of us are bent over laughing.

"There was a snorting deer alright, a deer named Gary!" Mark exclaims, and we laugh some more.

After packing up, we get back on route and ride for over an hour before we find a place to stop for breakfast. On more than one occasion we had casually talked about where this segment would end since we wouldn't be making it back to Metro Detroit as we had planned. The route on our touring maps heads south, then west toward the southwest corner of New York. That route continues through the edge of Pennsylvania, Ohio and Indiana as it bypasses Michigan. Our plan is to go off route through Canada.

Niagara Falls continues to come up as a good destination to end this segment. Ending there will allow us to make up that part of the trip in a long weekend and we're about three days ride from the falls, so that fits our schedule also. Gary says his father will most likely be able to pick us up and he'll call him to confirm. We have one more day on route, then the last two days we'll be off of it making our way with state maps as best we can.

We're back on the bikes under sunny skies. The temperature has warmed and jackets are stuffed away. The last couple of nights have been cold and today it's cooler. In a way it feels like the beginning of fall.

Mark rides up and asks, "How does your arm feel, where you got the tetanus shot?"

"Good, just a little sore, but not bothersome at all. And I changed the bandage on my knee this morning and the stitches look fine."

"That's good."

"Yeah, and all this road rash is scabbing over so it feels better," I say while twisting my arm so Mark can see. Then jokingly I say, "I'm ready to do a hundred miles!"

Gary is just ahead of us and quickly twists his head around. "You guys want to ride a hundred miles today? It's about time, you little girly men. You know, I was the only one up at the crack of dawn."

"That's because I didn't have a snorting-deer alarm clock to wake me," I retort and we all laugh.

The temperature remains mild throughout the afternoon and as evening approaches we're close to the point where we turn off.

We follow the touring maps approximately 8 miles into Red Creek as the route heads directly south, then break away to head east.

Not far from there, near Wolcott we find a campground. It's not that late but we had covered 72 miles and now that we're off route, only have state maps without much detail and no camping information, we decide to stop for the night. It seems like we frequently pull into camp near dark and for a change it's nice to be able to set up tents, take a shower and relax before it gets dark. There is a restaurant nearby that has a special on an all-you-can-eat spaghetti dinner with an enormous slice of lemon meringue pie for dessert, and that sounds good to all of us. Later we discuss the route ahead while trying to figure out the least traveled yet most efficient way to Niagara Falls.

The biggest challenge is finding a way to get through Rochester, the largest city we have come across so far. If we head south and try to bypass the congestion we'll be adding many miles to our route. Fighting our way through the city and being forced up on sidewalks, waiting for traffic lights and trying to figure out a way to cross expressways is not a good option either.

We'll hit Rochester this afternoon and try to bypass what looks like the most congested parts of the city without riding too far out of the way. This morning we'll be traveling through small towns, farms and forest. The day starts cool and sunny but becomes warm and increasingly cloudy. We are riding on the wide paved shoulder of a lightly traveled two-lane highway, single file. I'm out front and have fallen into a steady rhythm with an eye on the sign for the next turn. When I find it, I stop and grab the map to make sure this is our turn. Then I look back on the fairly straight road, down about a quarter of a mile before it curves and I can't see either Gary or Mark. I set down my bike and dig through my pannier for a quick snack. I figure that one of them had to take a quick bathroom break and they'll be riding up any minute.

I finish a miniature pack of M&Ms, stuff the wrapper in the outer pocket I put trash in, then pick up my bike and start riding back. I get to the point where the road curves and I still can't see them. Now I'm a little concerned. A few miles later I spot them in the distance walking through the tall brush on the side of the road. I can't figure out what they are doing. I ride up, "What's wrong?"

"I lost a cog on my rear derailleur," Mark says.

That doesn't make sense. "What?"

"I was riding along when my chain jammed. I came to a stop, got off, and noticed the lower cog on the rear derailleur and the axle bolt that holds it to the arm are missing. It couldn't have gone far but we've been looking for the last 15 minutes and can't find either one."

The rear derailleur places the chain on different sprockets to change gears but also takes up the slack so a chain that is one size can fit around many different size sprockets. There are two small, toothed wheels on the arm that the chain rides along. I had never heard of anybody losing one.

We brainstorm and find a stick, that if whittled down could be wedged into the hole where the bolt goes, but it doesn't seem like a great idea.

I join the search for the bolt and cog. The inertia of Mark's bike would have propelled the piece forward when it popped off, but it's possible that Mark didn't notice it at that exact moment and covered some distance before he stopped his bike. I walk down the road to an area a little further back than where Mark and Gary are looking.

"So you guys don't have an extra cog and axle bolt?" I say in a mocking disbelief while holding out my arms. We start laughing. "I'm really disappointed in you two!" And now, turning to Gary, "With all the community gear you're carrying, you couldn't bring upon yourself to pack an extra rear derailleur cog and axle bolt?"

While laughing, Gary defends himself by saying, "Well, if Mark would have bought a new bike for this trip, we wouldn't be in this situation."

Mark shoots back, "It's not the condition of my bike, it's that I'm not riding a Bruce Gordon Special!" And then adds, "How's that bottom bracket, Gary?"

We search for a while longer and find the bolt. When screwed into place, the chain glides along it without issue. Gary has a zip tie and suggests wrapping it around the bolt and cutting off the excess to reduce the friction, which seems to help.

We get back on the bikes and Mark delicately applies pressure until we're up to speed. At this point on the route there are no houses or buildings around and we aren't sure when we'll run into a bike shop, but for the time being it looks like Mark won't have a problem riding.

In the early part of the afternoon we come into a city bigger than what we had been used to as the sky is threatening rain. When it starts, we duck under the eave of a large grocery store and decide to wait a few minutes to see if the storm will blow over.

As we talk about finding a bike shop, across the large parking lot, to the left and on the other side of the street is an old house with a "Fix Bikes" sign in front of it. Gary points and says, "Hey, do you think that guy might have something?"

Gary and Mark eagerly head off in the rain while I stay behind. A few minutes later they come back with a story of a local eccentric who has a mountain of used parts and had something that fit Mark's bike.

"It works okay?" I ask Mark.

"Yeah, good."

"Did you try shifting?"

"Yeah, works fine. We don't need to find a bike shop."

I walk to the side of his bike to take a look at it. "Well it's a good thing you're not riding a Bruce Gordon Special otherwise you wouldn't be able to use those kind of parts." We all chuckle.

I point to a restaurant about 50 yards away and say, "Let's get something to eat and wait out this rain."

It comes down hard while we have a leisurely lunch. There are times when you need to ride in the rain but if we can avoid it, we will. Summer thunderstorms frequently come down hard for 15 minutes or so then clear right up and that's what we're hoping for.

The pavement is still wet when we start riding again but the rain had stopped. The congestion of Rochester crept up on us as roads grew increasingly wider and busier. Soon we're dodging traffic, being forced up on the sidewalk and biding our time at traffic lights that control streets with 6 or more lanes. At one light, as we're waiting for it to change, a man in a car pulls next to the curb and parks. He gets out and approaches us. "Where are you guys heading?"

We tell him we're on a cross-country trip heading back toward Detroit but our immediate destination is Niagara Falls. He is also a cyclist and starts talking about the cross-country trip he had taken. After we exchange bike stories we ask for directions. We tell him we're hoping to avoid the congestion and traffic and get through Rochester as quickly as possible. He thinks for a second and then tells us of a bike path that will take us off the streets and provide a scenic ride. As he points down the road and starts to give us directions, it sounds like it's a quite a distance from where we are. Considering we have no knowledge of the area and the route we're on isn't very pleasant, we decide to take his advice. To get to the bike path we'll have to ride south for quite a while then once on it, we'll head in a northwest direction.

We ride south for a long time and eventually feel we have gone too far out of our way. I'm thinking it would have been better to tough it out and fight the congestion by riding straight through the city. Yet once on the path, even if we had wasted some time getting there, there is an advantage to gliding along without the noise, frequent stops, dodging irritable drivers and riding on sidewalks. We wind through wooded areas and parallel the Erie Canal as we pass just a handful of people. It's far more pleasant.

Our maps don't show the bike path or canal and we aren't exactly sure where we are. We keep checking the cross streets when we come upon them looking for something familiar. Eventually we recognize a number from a sign, match it to a road on the map and are able to trace a route west. At this point we are out of the main part of the city and heading toward a less developed area. As the sun nears the horizon and facilities become more sparse, we look for a campground or motel. About 5 miles west of Rochester near the town of Spencerport we see a motel just off the road and get a room for the night. After we get cleaned up, we walk across the street to a restaurant. It had been one of our longer days, mileage-wise, and fighting the congestion of the city had been exhausting. After dinner we walk back to our room in the dark and while I'm interested in watching a little TV, I don't see much before I'm asleep.

We wake to cloudy weather with a cool, humid feel to the air and talk about the plan for today and tomorrow. Gary's dad will be on the

Canadian side of the falls around noon the following day so we just need to get close to the border today. We figure if we can cover 70 miles or so, the ride into Canada tomorrow will be short and easy.

After we pack up and have breakfast, we trace a series of back roads that lead us directly west toward the city of Lewiston. Throughout the morning, light showers turn on and off with regular frequency, which has us in and out of rain gear. Although it's damp and cool, the showers are brief and the temperature is high enough to prevent a chill.

The terrain is moderately flat and the shoulder on the road is wide enough to make us feel secure against the light traffic. We ride through small towns and past farms. My front tire still has a slight wobble, a remnant from the crash a few days ago but my injuries are healing nicely and hadn't prevented me from riding or impeded our forward progress.

This is the last full day of this segment and it's anticlimactic. I feel eager to get home, and am thinking ahead to the things I have to do when I get there, but conflicted with a desire to go on. At this point, we've come approximately 800 miles and I'm a little road weary. If we had planned to go on, perhaps I just need a rest day, a complete day off the bike for a change. And since I had already considered modifications to my gear, the means to implement those changes. The trip has been both challenging and fun, and with Mark and Gary there is always plenty of laughter.

Just east of Lewiston we find a campground. It had not rained for an hour or so and we were getting a little sun through a hazy sky but everything is still wet. As tents go up and gear is sorted, the last moments of daylight fail to take the cool damp out of the air. I notice there is firewood available and with some help from the white gas we're carrying for the stove, we soon have a healthy fire. The warm glow is welcome, it pushes back the dark and chases the dampness from the air. We start to recount the highlights and challenges of the trip while making jokes and poking fun at each other. We also talk about lessons learned and things we'll do differently next time. There is a sense of accomplishment with how far we've come while prevailing over various challenges, mixed with disappointment at coming up short of our goal. There is a sense of completion, conflicted with yearning to go on.

After breakfast the next morning we head south looking for a crossing into Canada and find the lightly traveled two-lane Whirpool Bridge. We line up side-by-side behind the last car and move forward with the traffic. When we get to customs we proceed one at a time and the process is quick and hassle free.

Gary's dad, Bob, said he'd be near the Skylon Tower in Queen Victoria Park, which is close to Horseshoe Falls, so we glide along River Road in a southerly direction until we find it. There is a large parking lot in the vicinity of the tower and when we get close we start scanning the area. Bob is driving a small, white motor home and soon Gary points and shouts out, "There he is." We pick up the pace as we zero in on our ride home.

Gary's wife, Gail, has also come and it's good to see both of them. We talk about the trip a little, then Mark, Gary and I stand together for some photos. After that, we load the bikes and gear. As we settle in and Bob starts the engine, Gail is eager to hear about the trip. The ride home is filled with laughter as we recount tales of snorting deer and bike malfunctions, great meals and odd characters, stitches and route finding issues.

On that back road in upstate New York we added Blue Highways to our name. It was painted on Mark's bike by its previous owner in reference to back roads that are colored blue on road maps. As such, we became known as the Blue Highways Cycling Elite in a manner that's more reminiscent of a Monty Python sketch as we search for laughter and adventure, than an organization of skilled, super bikers.

Interlude

During the winter Gary, Mark and I decide that we will stick with our original plan and start on the west coast the following year and work our way back to Michigan even though we still have to make up the distance between Metro Detroit and Niagara Falls.

As we work out the specifics, we continue to argue about whether it's necessary, on occasion, to ride after dark in order to cover enough miles each day to make our destination on time. There are two things that bolster Gary's point this time: with the mountainous terrain we will encounter, there is a good chance our miles-per-hour average will be lower, which will mean we'll need to ride longer each day to cover enough miles in this segment. Also, we'll have reservations for the trip home that have to be met.

I counter with better time management. On the last segment the sun came up around 6:30 a.m. which meant that we had roughly five and a half hours of daylight in the morning. Yet, before noon, we usually only covered between 10 to 20 miles. I argued we were wasting way too much time in the morning.

Again, we're at a stalemate.

After a few discussions we agree to move the next segment to mid-June so we can take advantage of the longer days. That way if we need to spend more time riding at the end of the day, we'll have more daylight to ride in. This seems like a good solution and I'm hoping it will work because I'm at the point where I'm tired of talking about this. I feel it's an unnecessary risk and a hassle to ride after dark. And it's irritating that the mileage issue only comes up at the end of the day when it's too late for other options.

Originally we chose the end of summer for the first segment because in Michigan, late spring/early summer can be rainy, cool and full of mosquitoes, black flies and other pests. I assumed that in other parts of the country the end, rather than the beginning of summer would be a better time to travel as well, but at this point having more daylight seems to take precedence.

There is another big logistical issue we need to work out. We will be starting in Anacortes just north of Seattle. Flying into Sea-Tac is the easiest way to get to that area but Anacortes is another 90 miles from the airport. We're uncertain if there is a direct route and even if there is, it will most likely be congested and not a very pleasant ride. We could take a shuttle to Anacortes, but Mark had read a story about biking on the San Juan Islands, a group of islands just off the coast near Anacortes and another idea emerged. There is a ferry from Seattle to the main island and another from the island to Anacortes. We come up with an alternate plan. We'll arrive in Seattle and spend the night there, the next day take a ferry to the islands and spend the day and night there, and the following day take a ferry to Anacortes to start the next segment of the trip.

When the final plan is set, we pick the day we'll meet in Seattle. Gary and Mark will fly in, while I had always wanted to take a long train ride so I'll do that. At the end of the segment, I'll take the train out of the town of East Glacier, Montana, on the eastern side of Glacier National Park and Gary and Mark will ride up the road a bit to the town of Cut Bank, rent a vehicle and drive it to Great Falls so they can catch a plane back to Detroit.

All three of us are making slight modifications to the gear we're carrying, leaving behind extraneous items, trying new things, and refining our clothing choices.

During the last segment, Mark and I shared a tent because Mark doesn't have one. I had only used that tent when I was alone, but with the two of us it seemed a little tight so I suggest we take my other one. It's bigger, and is advertised as a three-man tent, however, you could put three men in this tent much like you could fit four people in a phone booth. For the two of us it's a good size. It's a little taller, wider and longer, and the hexagon-shaped floor means there is some space for gear to the side of each of us. It weighs a little more but the extra space is worth it. Gary has a smaller, two-person tent. I think it's purposely called that because you couldn't, in good conscience, call it a two-man tent. But if he sleeps diagonally then it's a good compromise between weight and space.

The pockets on my panniers lay flat against the side and when the bags are full it's nearly impossible to put anything in them. I'm able to find a zipper and fabric that's similar to what the bags are made of and design a new pocket for one of them. I carefully tear off the old pocket at the seams and sew the new pocket, which has a depth of an inch and a half, in it's place. This is much better and is the new home for the tool kit, snacks and other small items.

The camera bag I had used as a handlebar bag wasn't such a great idea and I look for a hard plastic box to fit between the outposts of my widely spaced aero bar. Luckily I find something that seems built to fit. I put some foam inside so I can take my better camera, and make a map case out of some tough, clear vinyl that I Velcro to the top. The lid hinges open and snaps shut. I make an additional latch from Velcro so it's extra secure.

I'm interested in experimenting with plastic containers because even with rain covers on my bags there seems to be a little leakage in a heavy and prolonged rain. Further, not having to carry or deal with rain covers would be a bonus.

I keep thinking that a plastic box placed on top of my rear rack would not only be waterproof, but easier to use than the duffle I had for the foam pad, sleeping bag and tent. I would need something to carry these items, ideally with a little extra room. My foam pad is the least flexible in terms of size– I can squish my sleeping bag and tent into a container of any shape, but the rolled foam pad has a length and height that have to be accommodated.

I searched quite a few stores throughout the spring and couldn't find anything that was the size I was looking for, everything was either too big or too small. On the day before I leave, when everything else is set, I purchase two sturdy containers that look like a good compromise in the store, but once I try to position them on the rack, seem impossibly large. Panicked I would have to use the large duffle again, I'm determined to try something new even if it seems absurd and grab the smaller of the two containers with the idea I'll make it work. I want to mount the box longitudinally but the degree in which it cantilevers over the end of the rack makes it seem impossible to adequately secure. I set it on the rack crosswise. At nearly 34 inches long, this makes it about as wind resistant as a small parachute.

I stand in the garage, running out of time and think, There's just no good solution. I decide that a new dumb idea is better than an old dumb idea and I'll use the plastic container.

Strapping the box on the rack would defeat one of its benefits, the convenience of easily stashing something, like a jacket, or quickly accessing it. So I make a quick release plate for the bottom in order to secure it to the rack, allow easy access, and still be able to take it off at the end of the day. I'll also have a strap with me in case this doesn't work.

There is no time left to test it and I'm kicking myself for waiting until the last minute. At this point I'm committed to the idea whether it works or not and am hoping the wind drag won't be that noticeable.

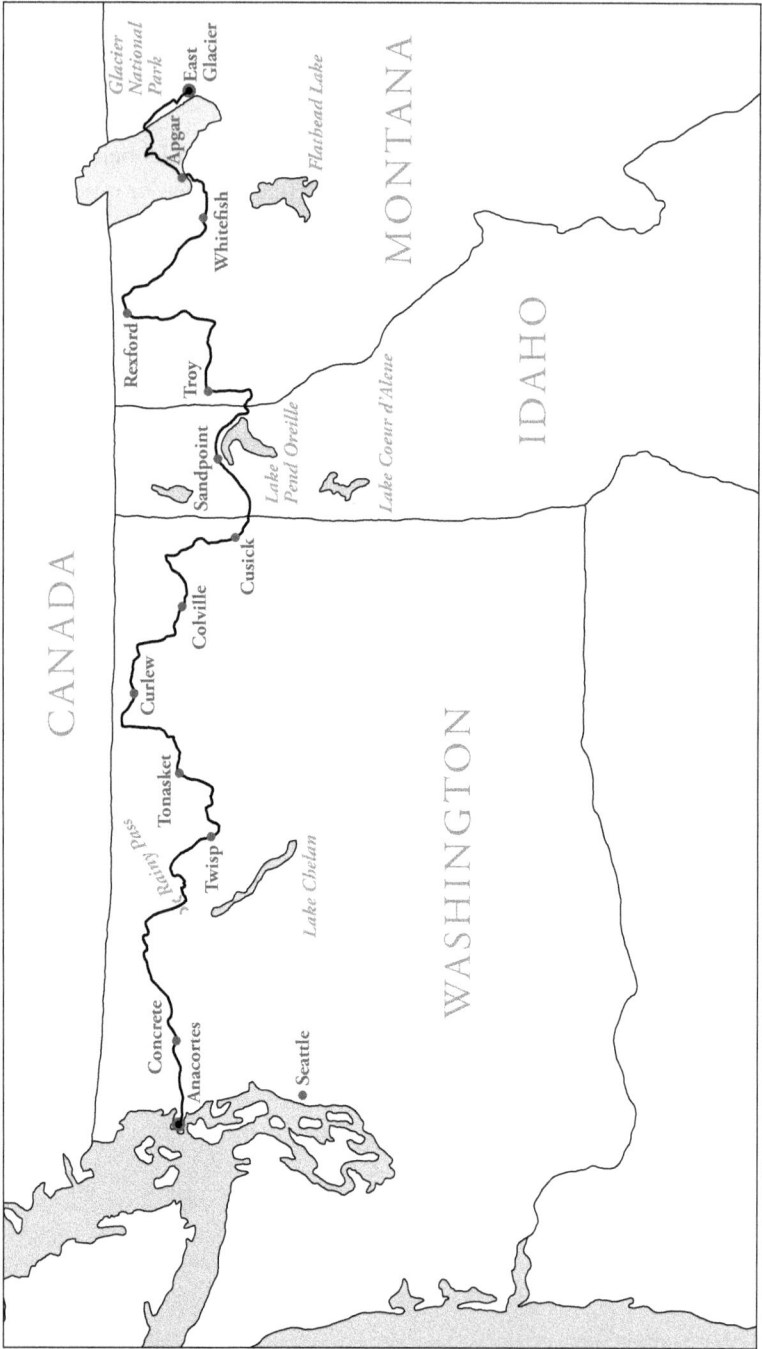

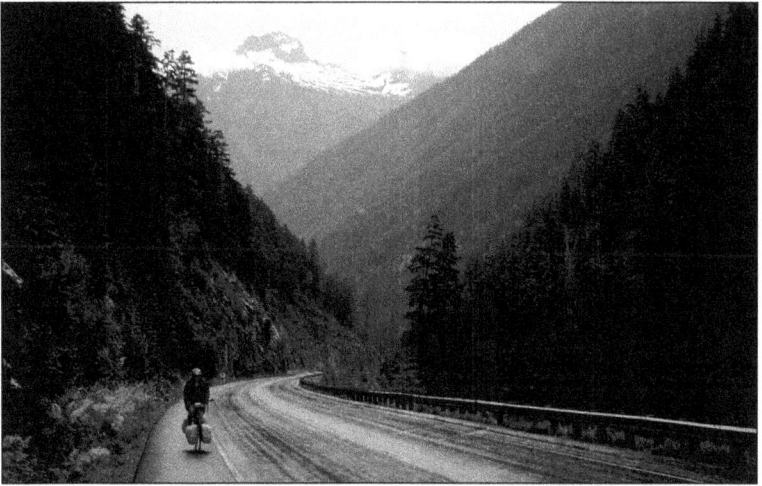

West

"It's better to take your bags off the bike because it will be quicker to go through customs," an employee of the tour boat operator says.

"Customs? We're not going to Canada," Gary replies.

"Then you are on the wrong boat."

Great. We haven't even started the next segment of the trip and we're already off route. Again, the irony of referring to our group as elite, in any manner, is laughable. Well, we can laugh about it only because we're able to get off the boat and catch the right one without delay.

I arrived in Seattle mid-morning and when I got off the train, found a cab for the short ride to our hotel. I check in knowing Mark and Gary won't arrive until mid or late afternoon, then unpack my bike and put it together. I unpack my other gear and place the things I had with me on the train in that box. This includes a blanket, small pillow, a couple of books, and things like that. I'm going to mail them ahead in care of the Postmaster and pick them up once I reach East Glacier for the ride home.

I decide to jump in the shower and get cleaned up, then double check my box of train supplies before taping it closed and addressing it. I roll the bike outside with the box strapped on and ride to the post office.

When I get back I lay down for a while and soon Mark and Gary are walking in the door. They stack up their gear and we trade travel stories for a few minutes before they start unpacking their bikes.

Gary carefully cuts his bike box open. It's a heavily reinforced, cardboard box that has an excessive amount of duct tape on it. He pulls the top off and I notice there are two separate compartments, one for the wheels and the other for the frame. Styrofoam triangles are wedged into the corners to stiffen and support the box, and the bike frame is attached to a specially built, wooden platform. Rolled up pieces of cardboard are placed crosswise to brace the sides in case something is set on it. He proudly shows off its features and it almost looks like a rough prototype for a new product.

Mark and I are laughing at what is obviously overkill.

"Your flight was shorter than the time you spent building this box!" I say, pointing out the irony of his project as we laugh.

"Did you use 4 or 5 rolls of duct tape on that thing?" Mark jokes, as he points to lines of duct tape that are perfectly parallel.

"If I was riding a bike like yours I'd be comfortable throwing it in a burlap sack," Gary replies as he carefully puts the lid back on and sets it aside.

"You know you have to throw it away now, unless you were thinking of strapping it to your back and carrying it all the way to Glacier," Mark says.

"Actually, I'm donating it to a worthy charity," Gary replies as we all laugh.

"I'm surprised you can part with it after all the work you put into it."

"That's okay Gary," I say with a smile on my face, "If it will make you feel better I'm sure we have an extra washcloth you can use as a rag to wipe the dirt off your box before you throw it in the trash." We're howling.

Gary diverts attention away from himself when he notices my new plastic container for the top of my rack. "What's with the big blue box?"

I can see myself stepping up as the brunt of the next round of taunting. "I wanted to replace the duffle I was using for the foam pad, sleeping bag and tent with something waterproof and easier to use."

"You're actually carrying that on your bike?" Mark asks with disbelief as much laughter ensues.

"Yeah, I know, it's not the best idea I ever came up with," I say and explain how it works and the trouble I had finding a container just the right size.

"It doesn't look very wind resistant," Gary surmises in a somewhat serious tone.

"Thanks, I never noticed that," I reply sarcastically as we all laugh hard. "I know, I might as well have a little parachute attached to my bike. But hey, these are the things I have to do so you guys can keep up with me!"

"Ooohhhhhh!" the guys groan as we start laughing again.

Gary retorts, "Well, if I wasn't carrying all the community gear..."

"Again, with that!" I cut him off as the guffaws continue.

"At least we'll have a bear-proof container for our food at night," Mark quips.

"And if we encounter a flood you could use it as a boat," Gary adds. This goes on for a while longer until the bikes are assembled and we're ready to ride in the morning.

Later, Mark and I spend a little time riding around the city and then all of us take a long walk and by the time we get back it's after dark.

We don't have to get up too early, so we don't. We take our time getting ready and leisurely sip coffee that's available in the lobby. I had picked a moderately priced hotel that's close to the dock where a number of ferries depart for a variety of destinations. It's less than a five minute ride to the ship.

Once we get on the right boat and depart, we go up top to get the best views of Puget Sound. It's hazy and overcast, but we can still see coastal mountains all around us. The temperature is mild but once underway, the wind is strong and cool. I zip up my jacket and flip up the hood.

We snake our way north past Bainbridge and Whidbey Islands until we get into the open area at the top of the Olympic Peninsula. The water is rougher here and the ship bounces around a bit. Luckily for both Gary and me, this part of the trip doesn't last too long and soon enough the ferry docks at Friday Harbor, on San Juan Island.

We disembark and while slowly riding with the crowd along the dock, I graze a pole forgetting the width of the blue box. It throws me off balance and I almost fall over. Gary sees me and we laugh. "Wide load."

Away from the dock, we ride into a lush, green countryside. All of us are happy to the point of giddy to be back on tour and anxious about the big climb into the Cascades. We casually glide along lightly trafficked roads riding side by side, joking and laughing.

San Juan Island National Historical Park is divided into two units, one on the north part of the island and one on the south. The island was disputed territory and peacefully occupied by both English forces in the north and American troops in the south until a resolution was agreed upon. We head toward the northern unit.

When we reach the old English encampment, we park the bikes and hike around, taking in some of the notable features. There is no specific agenda or miles to cover, so the day unfolds on it's own. Later, while we continue our tour of the island, we casually glide past what looks like numerous alpaca farms.

Toward the end of the day we decide to stay at a rustic campground and make our way there. We get a campsite and settle in.

Already, I'm enjoying the longer days and feel we made the right decision to move the trip to early summer. The daylight lingers into the evening as if it's hanging on for as long as possible before night moves in, pushing the light away until it's completely dark.

We ride back to Friday Harbor and arrive early enough to get something to eat before the ferry shows up. It's a short and calm ride to Anacortes as we slide between Shaw and Lopez Islands, then Blakely and Center Islands.

Once we dock, Gary pedals ahead and I see him turn left. That doesn't seem right. When I get to the intersection, I stop and look down at the map that's on top of my handlebar box. Mark pulls up and asks, "That's not the right way, is it?" I look up, shake my head and we start to laugh. "GARY! GARY!" we shout until he stops and turns around. We wait for him to get close and then I say, "The route is this way," as I motion with my thumb to the right. We all laugh as Gary rides by and Mark and I follow. Jokingly I say to myself, "Sometimes it's amazing we've been able to come this far."

We head in a southerly direction before picking up State Route 20, which is known as the North Cascades Highway, then head east and make our way through the congestion of coastal towns.

Because we would be traveling through some remote areas without convenient services, Mark brought a spare tire (we are all riding on the same size) in addition to the spare tubes and patch kits we all have. It seems a little excessive to me, but, as a perfect example of the self-fulfilling prophecy, Gary runs over something that slices his tire and tube to such an extent that he uses the spare. The gash in the tire is puzzling, it actually looks like someone made it with a sharp knife. We pull the wheel apart and in no time we are ready to ride again. Gary doesn't know what he ran over and backtracking a bit doesn't produce any answers either. But now Gary and Mark are absolutely convinced we need to carry a spare tire, while I'm still a bit skeptical. In a similar situation, I believe we could figure something out and hobble into a bike shop. My feeling is that I'd rather pare my load a bit, especially with all the climbing we'll be doing, and besides, a tire is an awkward item that's difficult to pack.

Past Burlington, we turn onto the South Skagit Highway that parallels the Skagit River and Route 20 but has less traffic. It's still overcast and cool but humid and damp too. The forest is dense and lush, there doesn't seem to be a bare square foot of dirt anywhere. The vegetation crowds the edge of the road and in many places the branches of tall trees have created a tunnel blocking out the sky.

The route has been fairly level and we're moving along at a good pace. Most likely we'll top our daily average concerning miles, which is a good psychological boost at the beginning of the trip.

In the early evening we pull into the town of Concrete and find a nondescript restaurant with an interesting buffet. I give it a try and find it outstanding. Like anyone, there are things I like and things I don't, but greeted by a buffet I like to put a little of everything on my plate because you never know when you are going to be surprised. And that includes vegetables, which I eat, but aren't my favorite. I never look at cauliflower and think, "Yum! I can't wait to try it!"

Potato salad, excellent. Three bean casserole, superb. Macaroni salad, amazing. A vegetable mix looks gruesome, but is delightful. There wasn't a single thing in the 12 or more dishes I tried that wasn't above par. We never pick overly fancy or expensive restaurants, in fact, we ate at some run down places and aren't above eating fast food either, so I suppose it's not surprising we haven't had very many amazing culinary experiences. When they came along it was a real treat.

At the end of the first day we settle in a dense and damp Rockport State Park after barely gaining 500 feet of altitude. It's nice that we are slowly easing into the climbing, but the elevation profile shows a sharp rise that will come sometime tomorrow. All of us feel we have the stamina to take it on, we're just unsure about how difficult it will be. For the next couple of days we'll climb from sea level to Rainy Pass, then over Washington pass at 5477 feet before making a lengthy descent. This will be the first of a few major climbs. There is mild apprehension among us since such an elevation gain will be the most challenging that we have ever faced and we're carrying an extra 40 or more pounds besides.

Our campsite looks like it's carved out of the forest. There is a distinct edge to it and where the vegetation begins, the brush looks impenetrable. We unload gear, set up the tents and hit the showers. By the time I get back it's almost dark.

Inside the tent I eat a granola bar and some chocolate. I write a few notes then look at the map and elevation profile again. By the time I shut off the flashlight and lay on my back in my sleeping bag, I'm amazed at how black it is. The overcast sky and thick forest choke out any light from the moon and stars. I pull my arm out and hold my hand a foot from my face but can't see it. I wriggle my fingers but still nothing. I pull it close until I see something and it's about two inches away. It's rarely this dark and it's a bit disconcerting. My eyes scan the tent and nothing is visible. I roll to my side, adjust the fleece jacket I'm using as a pillow, and soon I'm out.

"Let's stop over there," Gary says as he points to a small shack that's advertising food and coffee on the side of the road. There are outdoor tables with big umbrellas on top of a carpet of cedar wood chips and it's a nice, sunny morning. The sweet smell of coffee permeates the air as we walk through the door. I order just-made strawberry shortcake and a latte. We sit outside, the lone patrons, as the sun warms us. It's quiet and still. I pull the lid off my coffee and take a good whiff then scan the vibrant green countryside. "Living the dream," I say out loud. Mark and Gary chuckle through mouthfuls of shortcake.

A little farther down the road as we ride into town a sign says, Entering Marblemount, Last Major Services For 69 Miles. We have our second breakfast at a restaurant that serves buffalo and pick up some groceries at a nearby market. We need to carry enough food to get us through the next day or so. The grade is still mild but we know that later it will change.

Up the road, when we pass Newhalem the leisurely riding is over and the climbing begins in earnest under a hot and clear sky.

"Code Blue!" I shout out with Gary and Mark echoing my refrain until we sound like a trio of cattle rustlers trying to move the heard along. The day had started out sunny and cool but turned hot as we came to the most difficult climbing. The blazing sun combines with the long, slow, uphill slog, and soon sweat is running down my face.

Fortunately, the Cascades are truly spectacular. We are awe struck by the rocky snow-capped mountains that tower above dense, thick forests in vibrant shades of green. Around every corner is yet another dazzling view. We bike through a few short tunnels and over a bridge that spans the run off from a tall, thin waterfall. The metal grating allows us to look down into the gorge a hundred or more feet below us. As we climb, the vistas become more expansive.

We are slowly moving forward pushing hard with each stroke of the pedal. For hours we work those long uphill stretches toward Rainy Pass. This doesn't involve one straight uphill grind but a series of climbs, brief plateaus and minor descents as the road wriggles between the topography of the mountain. It takes some of the pleasure out of going downhill when you realize that you're only going to have to make up all the elevation you just coasted down before you get over the pass. But it's a nice break and feels good to move forward without pedaling. Overall, we are exhausted and often moving at a turtle's pace.

During a long uphill trudge I pull over to the side, catch my breath and while still straddling the bike reach down for my water bottle. Mark is just behind me, slowly rides up and stops. I twist my torso around and ask, "How are you doing?"

In a somber and serious manner Mark says, "Good." He reaches for his water bottle, takes a drink then wipes his forehead on his shirt-sleeve.

"So you're good with doing this hour after hour, day after day, for the next two weeks straight?"

Mark smiles and we chuckle. "I figure there's got to be a few nice downhill runs in there to break up the monotony."

"Nope. I looked at the map and it's all uphill from here on out." We laugh. "You feel okay?"

"Yeah, good. You?"

"Good. I was a little concerned with all the climbing on this segment, how we were going to adjust to it, but I think it's going to be alright."

"Yeah. Is Gary still up front?"

"Yeah, about a hundred yards or so."

"We should keep moving."

We take some more water then stand on the pedals to get the bikes rolling. I push down hard while pulling up on the handlebars as the bike creeps forward. After a few yards I settle into the seat. The sun is still hot but it's been cooling off a bit as we gain elevation and now clouds appear on the horizon.

An hour or so later the clouds move in and block the sun. These aren't high, it-might-not-rain clouds, these are thick, low, you're-about-to-get-wet clouds.

Most likely our first destination wasn't named Rainy Pass because it's sunny all the time, and true to its name, rain falls. Now it cools and the rain wear goes on. There is a chill in the air but within the rain shell it's steamy, along with stinky and damp from hours of sweating. The road is glossy and traffic virtually disappears. We're still ascending, it's tough riding and we're quietly grunting it out, none of us very happy.

When things turn miserable, we all know there is no use complaining. Even in tough times we try to make light of a situation and laugh together.

Gary is closely following Mark and I ride up next to them. I blurt out, "You know what I really like? Biking uphill for hours until you're nice and hot, and sweaty and grimy, then have to put on the rain gear because it's not only raining but the temperature dropped and you really can't ride without it, but you can't stand to wear it either. Then, as if that's not great enough, a semi comes along and sprays you with road grime. The only thing that would make this perfect would be a big old headwind just blasting down the mountain against us!"

I didn't get the belly laugh I was hoping for but it did lighten things up a bit.

Toward dusk it stops raining and we need to find a place in the forest to camp. We see a sign for the East Creek hiking trail and figure this might be a good opportunity. The trail descends sharply to the creek, then rises on the other side of a small bridge. The thick forest isn't making it easy to find a clearing and there doesn't seem to be any level ground, but eventually we find some spots for the tents.

This is one of the few times on the trip when we camp without access to a hot shower and after a day like today, I really feel I could use one. Instead, I walk down to the creek. It's flowing rapidly, so immersion is out of the question. When I step over the rocks on the bank and place a foot in the water, it's shocking how cold it is. Then I realize it's probably fed by snowmelt. I have a washcloth and do the best I can as my muscles tense and I grimace. I towel off, put on some clean cloths and head back.

After dinner we gather up some rope and our food and walk a distance from the campsite to hang it from a tree, out of the reach of bears and hopefully other animals too.

After dark, the river reveals it's complexity in a cacophony of gurgle, swirl, babble and roar that overwhelms all other sounds and dominates the night. I try to get as comfortable as possible on the uneven, rocky ground inside my sleeping bag and soon fade into unconsciousness.

In the morning the air is cool and damp but the sun is shining. We walk the bikes up the rough trail and back onto the empty gravel parking lot, then get back on the highway. It's early on a Sunday morning and traffic is nonexistent. The air is still and a serene quiet envelopes the mountains as the sun slowly moves upward over rocky peaks and brilliant green forest. We continue to climb in a methodical and rhythmic manner. I'm out front and leave Gary and Mark behind, traveling in my own private solitude.

Not having seen the guys in a long time, I pull over to the guardrail at the edge of the shoulder, grab some dried fruit mix and sit on the rail. It isn't long before they pull up and after a short break we start riding again. The air is cool but working our way uphill for so long I'm warm enough without a jacket.

When we reach Rainy Pass we stop for a break and take pictures.

In the distance, the tops of mountains are still mostly white. Even though it's June there are mounds of snow on the ground where trees prevent the sun from reaching them. This isn't unusual since this area can be buried in 10 feet or more of snow during the winter.

We're out of water but hoping to fill up at the nearby picnic area. Except we can't, because nothing is working. Luckily, there are a few groups of people enjoying the nice weather and we go begging for water. The first group we encounter generously fill our bottles. They ask where we're heading and we talk about the trip, recounting the progress we've made so far.

We continue working our way upward toward Washington Pass and now with a steady stream of hot sunlight on us, we're sweating profusely. During one of our breaks, Mark and I walk off the shoulder to a short, thin waterfall fed by snowmelt. I lean forward and the frigid water slaps the back of my head. I rub it around and over my face. When I straighten up I can feel the remainder run down my back.

By the time we get to Washington Pass we had been biking about four hours. We pose for photos at the sign marking the elevation then start the long ride downhill. For a day and a half we worked our way up and now we head down and down and down at excessive speed. It's hard to tell how long it lasts, it's such a blast to zip along without any effort. Almost 20 miles later we have to start pedaling and stop in the town of Mazama for lunch.

On the east side of the pass the climate and environment has changed in a rather abrupt way. We're leaving behind the tall craggy, snow-capped peaks, which are replaced by smaller, rounder mountains and hills. It's drier here, you can feel it in the air and see it in the hard-packed, dusty soil. There are fewer trees, and brush grows closer to the ground. The former predominately green landscape is now supplemented with various shades of brown.

We find a place with carry out and eat at a picnic table in the shade while a dry, warm breeze blows around us. Checking the elevation profile on the map I find that we've lost about 3200 feet from the top of the pass and we'll gradually lose more as we pass through Winthrop and Twisp. Then it will be another steep climb to Loup Loup Pass.

The afternoon is hot and sunny with no shade and while gravity is mostly on our side the wind has kicked up dramatically, making a leisurely ride a bit of a struggle. The air doesn't seem to know where it's going and comes at us from different directions, most likely directed by the surrounding hills and mountains.

It's remarkable how dry and dusty it is here, seemingly a short distance from the saturated environment we just left behind. Cool, rainy and lush gave way to a hot, arid and sparse landscape that's reminiscent of the southwest at times. For the last few days the color palette consisted of highly saturated greens with blue-gray rock above. Now it's dominated by dark yellows and browns with low scrub and widely spaced trees.

We ride into Winthrop, and find the bike shop. Mark gets another tire and Gary gets one too plus a new bike seat. He had been complaining that his old seat was uncomfortable to a degree that Mark and I are glad he's replacing it, even though it's become something we joke about. We leave and bike another 8 miles or so and find a campground outside of Twisp. Nearby is a place where we can get pizza and it's delivered to our campsite by a guy driving a golf cart. We eat and settle in for the night.

We wake to sunny skies and soon start the steep climb to Loup Loup Pass, approximately a 2500 foot elevation gain. Compared to what we've come through, the climb seems easier. Not that it is easy, we still slow to a pace that's barely faster than a casual jogger, pushing down on each stroke, pulling up against the handlebars or zigzagging when the traffic is light on the steep sections. But more so, I believe, because our bodies and muscles are adjusting to this kind of taxing routine. It's still a grind, but I don't feel as exhausted or have the sense of trepidation I had in the beginning.

The air is warm but clouds move in and block the intense brilliance of the sun, which is a welcome relief since we are sweating heavily. As we ascend, it's greener and there are more trees but mixed in with large patches of yellowed terrain.

On the other side, the descent is steep at first, but seems to taper off and go on for quite a long time as we glide along with minimal pedaling. I keep anticipating the end, thinking we used up whatever elevation we had gained, but it's a pleasant surprise to keep coasting. It's still warm and overcast which is the perfect accompaniment to the terrain.

I sit up and take my hands off the handlebar, lean back and place them on the edges of the big blue box. For a second I consider a back for my seat like a reclining chair, and posts that stick out from the front fork to rest my feet on, that would also allow me to steer, then laugh at the ridiculousness of such an idea. Besides, I would never hear the end of it from Gary and Mark even though I know they would be secretly jealous, or so I tell myself.

As we come into Okanogan our leisurely descent is over and we stop for lunch. I see Gary open a small bottle and shake out a couple of Motrin. "You okay?" I ask.

"Yeah," Gary says with more of an irritated look on his face than a painful one. "My knee is bothering me a bit."

After lunch the sun comes out as we head north and soon it feels like it's in the 90's. There isn't a bit of shade and compared to the weather and climate we had been used to, the sun is blistering. The landscape is still dry and sparsely vegetated, mainly with short brush.

Past Omak, we are still on State Road 20, the same road we've been on almost exclusively since Anacortes. Occasionally we pass farms with irrigated green pastures but the surrounding hills have much less growth and it's mostly brown and withered ground cover. Trees dot the landscape and cluster along the banks of rivers. The countryside is a mixture of golden hues with a smattering of green.

For the rest of the afternoon we experience a relatively level route, however the wind grows strong and thwarts our forward progress. If the big blue box is acting like a parachute I don't notice the effects. I'm not having a problem keeping up with the guys and it doesn't feel any more difficult riding in this wind than others I've encountered without it. Of course, the way to measure it's effect would be to mount it longitudinally or take it off without reducing the weight of it's contents, but I'm just not interested enough to try anything. I'm sure there is some negative consequence, but it's not a big deal. I know I need a better solution and I'll come up with something for the next segment.

By the time we arrived in Tonasket, my skin is an intense shade of red. I pull up my shirtsleeve and see a pasty white underneath. "I really need to get some sunscreen," I say out loud to no one in particular.

We find a restaurant for dinner and afterward a place to camp.

Sometimes campgrounds are remote and our site is secluded. Other times it seems like we are camping in someone's backyard. This one is like that. But it doesn't matter, we have access to a bathroom with showers and a place to pitch the tents. The fact that an ice cream parlor is part of the encampment had absolutely no bearing on the decision to stay there. Really. Swear to God. (Okay, maybe a little).

"Man, did you hear that screaming, drunken woman last night? I could barely get to sleep," Gary said the next morning. Even though Mark and I were camped within 15 feet of Gary's tent we never heard her.

It seems like every third night or so Gary has a story of something that prevented him from achieving sound sleep. We're sympathetic to a point, Gary's snoring sometimes prohibits him from getting a good night's sleep, which then makes him susceptible to other disturbances. But we also can't pass up an opportunity to poke fun either, because sometimes the reasons seem ludicrous.

"Yeah, I couldn't get to sleep either because there was a streetlight that was shining through my tent window like a beacon," I joke.

"And I couldn't get to sleep because there was a snorting deer right outside my tent," Mark exclaims. At that point I'm sure Gary was sorry he had said anything and we're all laughing hard.

Just as we came into Tonasket last night, a sign informed us Sherman Pass is closed. Heavy rain had caused mudslides that damaged the road and we have to take a detour. This morning we are realizing the impact of this. As we look at the map we see the alternate route heads north, then west, then south to reconnect with the road we're on. We'll have to ride an extra 50-60 miles. This is cause for a lengthy discussion over breakfast about our schedule and the possibility of missing our connections to get back home. We had planned this trip around our 65 miles-a-day average, which we established on the first segment. Right now we are a little below that because the uphill miles have slowed us down a bit. When you add the few extra miles we need to make up to the detour, we're looking at mileage that accounts for nearly an entire day, or more. The gist of our discussion is how to make up the extra miles. Since we had moved this segment from late summer to early summer and are riding with the longest days of the year, we have more time to bike each day. Also, Sherman Pass is the highest elevation we'll reach in Washington and based on how long it took us to cross Rainy, then Washington Pass, if the alternate route has less climbing, it's possible that it might be almost as quick as heading over the pass.

All of us agree we can make up the time a few miles a day depending on riding conditions and are confident we will end the trip on schedule, but it's a reminder of how quickly things can change, and the effect those things can have on a trip.

We bike along the relatively level road for quite a while until we start the slow and steady climb toward Wauconda Pass. "Code Blue!" Gary shouts out as we downshift into the lowest gear and push hard on the pedals. We won't get to the detour until sometime this afternoon because we figure it will take a good part of the day to tackle the nearly 3000 foot elevation gain to the pass, where we have to turn off.

I'm routinely alternating between the drop handlebar, the straight bar and the aero bar, as I had been doing since the start of the trip. The aero bar requires a riding position that seemed awkward at first, but now that I'm used to it, I find it comfortable. On the fast descents I still use the straight bar exclusively because it offers the most control and leverage, but otherwise rotate between positions without thinking about it. Although a bit heavier than a single bar this combination is successful at preventing tension in my upper back, and sore wrists and numb fingers, and I'm enjoying the variety. Mark and Gary have the traditional drop handlebars and can grip the top part of the bar near the stem or the lower part, but they still experience some issues. At different times throughout the trip, Gary experimented with rotating his handlebars to varying degrees until once they were as vertical as he could make them, giving himself a more upright riding position. Each time he adjusted them, he'd ride for a while in that position then try something else.

Just short of the Pass, we stop at a junction and have lunch at a small café. This is the place where the detour starts and after we eat, we head north on Toroda Creek Road instead of directly east toward Sherman Pass.

It's nice to end the climbing a bit earlier than we thought. The weather is warm and overcast, and it seems like we spend an unusually long time gliding downhill. These conditions make for a nearly perfect afternoon that takes the sting out of having to ride so far out of the way.

Eventually the road curves east and at this point we are so far north that it looks like we're only eight miles or so from the Canadian border. We are now riding parallel to our route and the first part of the extra miles didn't seem to take up too much time.

As we've made our way east from the dry environment just this side of the Cascades, the climate has become less arid and the landscape slowly turns back to green from yellow and brown. Instead of spotty trees that dot the landscape there are large clusters that share the land with open fields. At higher elevations we ride through the kind of forests we are used to in Michigan and out east, though they are not quite as dense. It's not as damp and lush as the terrain west of the Cascades, but isn't as dry, yellow and sparse as the area just after those mountains either.

In the early evening we ride into the small town of Curlew. From the road we see a plain, gray, concrete-block building without windows. The sign above the double doors says, Restaurant, and, Lounge. The design seems a little odd for a restaurant but we stop and inquire. Inside it's nice and we decide to stay for dinner.

There is a campsite nearby but it's not that late so Gary makes a faint argument to keep riding. It seems like we're coming up short on miles every day and must be considerably behind schedule, but a quick calculation shows we have averaged 61 miles a day. This isn't great, especially considering the extra distance from the detour that's been added to the trip, but it won't be a big challenge to make that up. To bolster Gary's argument we have only covered 60 miles today, but we are also off route and have no idea when we'll come across the next campground. The elevation profile on the maps show the most severe climbing will soon be over and next week the terrain will be moderately level. This will mean our miles per hour and miles per day will most likely be greater. We decide to stay for the night.

For breakfast we head back to the restaurant we nicknamed, The Bunker. After we eat, we continue east and not surprisingly, encounter a long steep climb as we ride over the Kettle River Range. This is simply the northern part of the range that we would have crossed if Sherman Pass had been open.

The day started cloudy and cool with rain threatening, but we were hoping to avoid it. As we begin the climb and our pace slows the air feels damp and has that earthy smell of rain in it.

Before we get to the pass we're wet. We were already damp from the uphill struggle but as rain falls, it forces us to put on rain gear. In spite of miraculous high-tech fabrics that tout waterproofness and breathability, there isn't a fabric that can prevent the damp, clammy feeling when it's pouring rain and you are working against a long uphill climb. The temperature has dropped, so when we stop for a break it doesn't take long to cool off and develop a chill. It's cold and miserable as we dig in and climb to the top.

Once on top we stop for a short break. When Mark, then Gary, take off I wait about 15 seconds to put some distance between us. If someone falls down unexpectedly, none of us wants to ride over him and crash too. Besides, coming to a stop at 35 mph or more if someone needs help will take some distance.

Usually the descent is something to look forward to but as I take off, rain stings my eyes and I lightly apply the brakes to try to control my speed out of fear the wet pavement will send me skidding across the road and over the edge or slam me into the ground. Mark and Gary are waiting at the bottom.

The junction is just up the road and we make a right turn, heading south. I look at the state map I have and figure we'll be back on route before the end of the day. We're now on the more heavily trafficked Route 395, but that's in comparison to the roads we had been on where we might not see a car for 15 minutes or more. The shoulders are good and we plod along in the rain. The storm is erratic. The rain stops for a while but starts up again, then turns off, then on.

Toward the end of the afternoon we get back on route as we turn east and cross the long, thin Franklin Roosevelt Lake. It's been cool and rainy all day and we feel chilled and soggy. The ride through Kettle Falls and into Colville is moderately level as we make our way over small hills and through light traffic.

We find a campground on the outskirts of town. It hasn't rained in an hour or so but everything is wet and we set up tents on soggy grass. There is a break in the clouds as twilight sets in but it's only a small clearing and heavy low clouds still dominate the sky. I tell the guys I'm riding into town to look for a drug store and ask if they need anything. I knew I'd run out of toothpaste because I forgot to get some before I left but figured I'd just stop somewhere along the route and replenish. It's a short trip and without the weight of the gear on my bike I accelerate like a rocket. I find a place and once inside grab some snacks too. It's dark as I ride back and when I get to our campsite, line up my bike with Mark and Gary's and run the cable lock through the bench of the picnic table to secure the bikes.

Although it looks as if it might clear, it rains hard and long through the night.

Everything is saturated but at least it's not raining. I pack up my gear, grab the zipper tab for the door and in a sweeping arc, the damp fabric falls to the side. I delicately scooch through the opening, trying not to touch the wet tent. I load my gear, Mark does the same, and we break down the tent. Just before I'm ready to jump on my bike, I use my hand to squeegee the rain off the seat, then a tissue to wipe it dry. In town we find a place to eat then get back on route.

The sky has been overcast since we woke but we're hoping the rain has moved on. Not far down the road the sun does peek out and eventually we have extended periods of sun even though the clouds refuse to move on.

Soon we start another long uphill climb over the Selkirk Mountains. The elevation gain is approximately 1500 feet, which on paper, seems moderate compared to what we've been experiencing. While that doesn't make the climb easier we are relived it won't last as long as some of the others.

In spite of the sunshine the air is cool and that makes the climb a bit more tolerable. The road curves back and forth as we crawl along but with the shorter climb we don't get the expansive views that we see higher up.

Gary cries out, "Code Blue!" after we hit a short plateau then start climbing again, not that we need to be reminded to downshift. Sometimes I think Gary just needs to yell out, like a coyote barking at the moon. The reason I know this is because I often feel the same way.

Before we get to the top, the clouds thicken and we have to put on the rain gear again. The rain is light and I leave the jacket mostly unzipped for extra ventilation. Also, I loosen the Velcro on the wrists and get some cool air to ride up my arms.

Because heavy rain throughout the spring has caused numerous mudslides, we've ridden through a few areas of road construction. Sometimes we just snake our way over gravel and around some heavy equipment but this time we have to wait with the other traffic for our turn to ride on the single lane road. We've reached a plateau and while standing there the raindrops turn solid and we're pelted with hail. It's cool, but not that cold, and now that it's summer it seems odd to the point that we all start laughing. It only lasts a minute or so then turns back to rain, and soon it's our turn to move forward.

At the top we take a short break. The rain has stopped and the road looks dry but the clouds still hang overhead. When we're ready to descend I see a road sign that says '6% GRADE' but has a picture of a truck on what looks like a downward, 30 degree angle. I'm guessing the 6% grade is a more accurate description of the road but that makes it seem like the toddler roller coaster at an amusement park. Once we start the descent it's anything but, and speed builds as I brace myself and lean back and forth through the curves. The velocity of the descent always means it's going to be over much quicker than the climb, but it's still a bit of a let down when you realize the fun part is finished, the road levels off and you have to start pedaling again.

We turn north in Tiger, and just before we reach Ione, jog east over the Pend Oreille River and head directly south, paralleling the river.

Nothing seems to connect in a straight line. Traveling 20 miles east might mean riding that far north and south for a total distance of 40 miles. With our concern for making our destination on time it's discouraging to look at the map and see that we are heading almost directly south for the next 30 miles. This thought is tempered with the realization that the total miles we have to cover on this segment account for this kind of travel and we determined the number of days needed to get to our destination based on that.

The rain seems to move on and we are getting longer periods of sunshine. The route has leveled off and just when we think we can pick up our pace a strong headwind fights against us. I hunker down and dig in as I rotate between the aero bar and the drop handlebars. Between the climb, the rain, and now the headwind, today is turning out to be tougher than it first appeared. Still, there's a chance the wind might die down or shift directions.

Nearly 30 miles later we push into Cusick having battled the wind all the way. We find the campground and get set up then order pizza from a store across the highway that has a limited take-out menu.

Over dinner we look at the maps and the elevation profile again. We're close to the Idaho border now and from here to Glacier National Park there will only be minor hills to climb and we'll have time to make up the mileage we're behind.

The next morning is typical of our routine: Wake to daylight and cool temperatures and slowly rouse from the sleeping bag while quickly reaching for the fleece jacket. Determine what gear is needed for the morning and cram small and medium size items into panniers. Forsake the sleeping bag from around waist and legs and push it into its stuff sack and roll up and secure the foam pad. Place everything just outside the door. While sitting inside the tent, with feet outside, put on shoes. Load panniers and gear on the bike and disassemble the tent. The fly comes off and is folded, tent poles are released from their moorings at the base, slid out and folded, the tent body is folded, rolled and packed.

The fly and poles are put away when I kneel down and bend forward to fold the tent. Involuntarily I blurt out, "Aaahhhhg," as torso muscles are tightened and I wince in pain. I lose strength in the muscles that are holding my back at that precise angle and pitch forward practically hitting my head on the ground while rushing to reach my hands forward to cushion the blow.

"What happened?" Mark asks.

Bent forward with my head near the ground I say, "It felt like I got stabbed in the back and then I didn't have the strength to hold myself up." I push up on all fours like an animal. "Oh, that's painful."

I walk my hands off of the tent and Mark folds it up. The pain quickly subsides while I kneel there immobile, but I'm afraid to get up.

"Are you okay?" Mark asks.

"Yeah, I think so."

"You know what will fix you up? Motrin!" Gary says laughing. "I've got enough for the whole group." We all laugh. Gary was having some issues with his knee and now his Achilles tendon, and it seemed like he had been taking Motrin regularly since the third or fourth day.

"I've got aspirin, in fact plenty of it," I say. "You know, just in case you need some."

"No, I'm good."

"Just saying I got you covered. I'm always looking out for the group, you know, carrying my fair share of the community gear and all, cuz that's the kind of guy I am."

We're all laughing again.

I push myself into a standing position but, "Eeech!" comes out like a grunt as I cringe and jerk forward, bent at the waist.

"What's wrong?" Mark asks.

"I can't seem to straighten up." My upper body was leaning forward about 30 degrees.

"Are you okay?"

"Ummm... I pause for a few seconds. "Yeah. I'm not in pain, standing like this but I can't straighten up. I think I'll be able to ride, though."

Gary pops some Motrin. "Are you sure you don't want any of these?"

"I think I'm going to wait a bit and see how it goes."

I delicately swing a leg over the bike, stand on the pedal and once it starts to move forward place my elbows on the aero bar. So far, so good.

"If you had a bike seat like mine I'm sure you'd feel a lot better," Gary says laughing. I can't help but laugh too. Since Gary bought his new seat he had made a joke out of telling us how much he liked it, sometimes six or seven times a day, and although Mark and I were sick of hearing about it, we couldn't help but laugh every time Gary brought it up.

"I know you appreciate my humor. You feel better, don't you?" We're laughing in spite of our physical ailments.

It's cloudy and cool. The terrain is mostly level with only small hills but we have to fight a strong headwind again, however this time it seems to ebb and flow as we travel in a mostly southeast direction along the river.

After a while we stop for a short break. My back is fine while riding, but when I get off the bike I straightened up out of habit, and then, "Eeech!" and quickly bend forward. I can stand and walk while slightly bent at the waist but I can't straighten up without pain. Gary is now at the point where he is hobbling around trying not to bend his ankle too much.

"I might just have to leave you old guys by the side of the road as I finish this tour by myself," Mark jokes.

"I'd be doing okay if I wasn't carrying all the community gear," Gary exclaims, as we laugh hard.

When we get to Newport, on the border of Washington and Idaho, we stop to do laundry, then find a place for lunch. I often forget that I can't straighten up and try to do so, sometimes in mid sentence. "Pass me that, eeech! detergent, will ya?" "Hey, there's a table, eeech! over there."

After lunch we cross into Idaho. It had been overcast for most of the day and we were hoping to avoid rain but it was to no avail. It only lasts about a half an hour but it's cold and hard and the clouds don't clear after. Later in the afternoon as the sky darkens and rain looks imminent, we temporarily seek shelter at Round Lake State Park. It comes down again, another cold, hard rain of short duration, and there is a tangible chill in the air that lingers.

It isn't long after we leave the State Park, that we're routed onto a paved bike path that goes on for miles and leads us straight toward Sandpoint. We don't pass anyone until we get close to the city and then cross a long bridge that spans Lake Pend Oreille. The bridge must be about a mile and a half long and offers great views of the surrounding mountains and lake. A blanket of gray and dark blue clouds cover the sky just above the mountaintops. The air is cool and damp and it looks like we might get rained on at any minute.

Once in Sandpoint, feeling chilled, we spot a coffee house and are drawn to it like a magnet. We could use a break and a place to warm up. Dismounting, Gary walks with a hobbled gait and I'm bent forward as we both make our way into the coffee house: Frankenstein followed by Groucho Marx.

We're in no hurry to jump back on the bikes as we sit in cushy chairs and sip hot coffee. Since it's getting late we decide to find a place to eat, then bike a bit farther to a campground we find on the map.

We set up at a place just north of Hope, Idaho, ending the day with nearly 70 miles accomplished, higher than our average and what we planned on, but still a little behind schedule because of the detour and coming up a bit short on the days of steep climbs. We talk about this frequently and it's become quite tiring. It is definitely one of the drawbacks of doing a trip in segments where reservations for transportation back home have to be met. Still, we need to make up some miles that we're behind and over the next couple of days have the opportunity to do so as long as our health issues don't escalate.

Breakfast is in a nicely refurbished hotel restaurant in Hope with big windows overlooking Lake Pend Orielle. It's sunny, a bit on the cool side, and we take off knowing that we'll cross into Montana later. Psychologically this seems like a notable landmark and proof that we are making progress toward our goal even though it feels like we are spending as much or more time going up and down and north and south as we are heading east.

The route skirts along the edge of the lake then breaks as we ride through Clark Fork. We had passed few buildings and most likely would not see much civilization for the next couple of days.

When we cross the border, we lose an hour and set the clocks on our electronic speedometers back. Knowing the right time will be important for making connections with our transportation back home, but on a daily basis I rarely knew what time it was and didn't care. For that matter I didn't know the date or even the day of the week, usually.

Riding through sparsely populated areas means that we often have a hard time finding a restaurant. We had been casually looking for something for a while when we finally come upon a bar that looks like it serves food. We enter the gravel parking lot and notice a number of motorcycles and a few guys standing near them off to the left. We pull up next to the door and set the bikes to the right of it, close to the building.

As we walk inside, the first thing I notice is the crunch underfoot. There are so many peanut shells on the floor it's impossible to take a step without walking on some. Next, the only other patrons are 15 or so bikers, of the motorized kind, clad in black leather. It's a little disconcerting but we find a booth in the corner and try to pretend we're invisible.

After looking at menus, the waitress takes our order and leaves. Suddenly a pig appears. The top of his back is taller than the height of our table and he's seven feet long or more. The pig walks past us and rather aimlessly roams between the other tables oblivious to everyone, and vice versa, except us who can't stop staring until he disappears through a doorway near the back.

At this point we are enjoying the eclectic atmosphere almost in a voyeuristic way until one of the bikers approaches our table and without any kind of greeting, gruffly blurts out, "How much did your bikes cost?"

Not liking where this conversation might go, we are hesitant to answer. The three of us look at each other while trying to determine if these guys are hard-core and looking to start something or just good old boys in costume.

Trying to evade the question, I say, "Depending on the quality of the bike you could probably get something as cheap as..."

The biker impatiently cuts me off, "NO. How much did *your* bikes cost?"

Instantly my mind calculates the worst-case scenario. If these guys want to steal our gear there is little we can do to prevent them, we are in a place that is a little too remote and they far outnumber us. I want to say my bike cost $19.99 but that would be ridiculous to anyone. Then I wonder if this is a prelude to a fight. I'm not a big guy, but if someone starts to throw punches I'm not going to let him pummel me like a speed bag. Besides, there is no way in hell we can out run them.

A few seconds of silence pass before I say, "My bike cost about seven hundred, the racks and bags cost around two fifty. Plus there's all the camping gear and clothing and I have no idea what I spent on that stuff."

Just as gruff, he says, "Huh," and walks away.

We look at each other as if we had just dodged a bullet, though don't know if we were really in any danger at all.

The rest of lunch is uneventful and soon we're gliding through the Cabinet Mountains where not only services are sparse but also inhabitants. The route now heads almost directly north. It's cloudy and a bit cool, so we have light jackets on. It's actually nice biking weather. The grade is moderate and small hills are quickly run up. We ride abreast for long periods because traffic is so light.

When we hit the junction for Highway 2 we head left and off route about two miles into the town of Troy for dinner. There's a campground in the area and we stay for the night. The terrain has been relatively flat in comparison to what we've come through and we had another day where we clocked more miles than our average.

Over breakfast we scan the route ahead. Our maps warn us: IT IS 66 MILES BETWEEN LIBBY AND EUREKA AND SERVICES ARE EXTREMELY LIMITED. CARRY EXTRA FOOD AND WATER BETWEEN THESE TOWNS.

Libby is up the road a ways but after checking the mileage it doesn't look like we'll be stranded. We top off our water bottles and check our food supply before taking off.

It takes us a couple of hours to get to Libby then a couple more to get to Libby Dam. We had been riding on the north side of the Kootenai River, then the west side as it turned north, and are now directed over the top of the dam to the other side.

We stop for some sight seeing and a long break. I take a walk through the visitor center on the west side of the dam and then bike over the top to where the observation tower is. I climb up a few flights of stairs to a view of the long and narrow Lake Koocanusa, which we'll be riding along for the next 50 miles or so.

The dam is a stark visual contrast to its surroundings. It was built with smooth surfaces and sharp angles. Nearly every part is made of concrete, which creates a dull gray, monotone façade. From the edge of the dam the dark blue of the lake, with shades of green framing it, extends out to the low hanging gray blue clouds. From a distance, the landscape is fuzzy like velvet. Trees and brush cover the rolling hills and mountains. The wind creates ripples in the lake and rustles the trees. The terrain is vibrant, alive. The dam stands stoic, staid, resolute.

The road along the lake is a steady routine of climb and glide. We climb to great views of the long and narrow lake then glide into the thick forest. None of the hills are very tall and the descent is helpful in building momentum to rise above the next one. Thicker clouds move in and we have an intense burst of rain that doesn't last long. The thick cloud cover stays with us, but occasionally we get spotlights of sun. We are anticipating more rain but it doesn't come and eventually the pavement dries and humidity drops.

As the day wears on, in spite of the picturesque landscape, climb and glide becomes quite tiring. Because it takes more time to climb to the top of a hill than it does to descend it, we've spent far more time climbing than gliding. As the map predicted we saw no services and few buildings, and at times it seems like we have the road to ourselves.

I was concerned about my back and afraid the condition would worsen but I've seen steady improvement to the point where I'm just a little stiff now. Gary's Achilles tendon is still bothering him but he doesn't seem to be hobbling around like he was. Gary has frequently mentioned some body ailment or another throughout the trip but it's hard to know how much pain he's in because it never seems to keep him from laughing, or taunting and poking fun at Mark and me.

We stop for a break and I see Gary shake out a couple of tablets from a small bottle. "How are you doing MoBo?"

Gary looks at me, "What?"

"Oh that's my new nickname for you, MoBo, short for Motrin Boy." The three of us laugh hard. If I thought Gary was suffering I wouldn't tease him about this, but he seems to be doing better.

Gary fires back. "I think, eech! I'll be alright, eech! I'm actually, eech! feeling better," Gary says mocking me and my sore back. We can barely stand up we're laughing so hard.

We arrive in Rexford in late evening and while the population is barely over 100 it's large enough to have a campground with a bar next to it where we can get dinner.

I check my odometer and it shows we ended the day 23 miles above our daily goal. It feels like it. It's good that we clocked the extra miles but I'm exhausted.

For a good part of the day we've been heading in a mostly northern direction. Over dinner I look at the map and see that again, we're barely eight miles from the Canadian border. Tomorrow we head south, southeast, as we work our way through the terrain.

Tents are set up, showers taken and by the time it's dark I'm out.

The next day as we are breaking camp, Gary complains about a guy in a camper set up near us. He was watching, I Love Lucy, reruns late into the night and woke Gary up. He is distraught telling us this, but as soon as Mark and I smile at yet another, "I couldn't sleep..." story, Gary pauses and without another word, all of us are laughing.

We ride eight miles into Eureka to find a restaurant because the bar next to our campground isn't open for breakfast. There are a few more towns on our route today but we are still riding in a remote area. The map lists the population of Eureka at 1,043, the upcoming Fortine at 400, Stryker 62 and Olney 250.

It's a sunny day and after breakfast it feels like it's going to be a lot warmer than it has been. We set our sights on Whitefish and according to the elevation profile on the map, we'll gain about 500 feet early on, then level off.

Throughout the morning there are sporadic climbs as we gradually ascended to a new plateau. After numerous days of cool and cloudy, or mostly cloudy, now the sun is out in full force and we are sweating heavily.

If there was a restaurant on route for lunch we didn't see it and instead, take a few extended breaks to stretch our legs and eat snacks. I like dried fruit, especially pineapple and apricots and when I find it in the store, usually get a mixture of different things. Occasionally I'll pack gorp, a blend that generally starts with a base of raisins and peanuts. Frequently I'll carry some kind of granola-type bar, but I have a soft spot for brown sugar cinnamon Pop Tarts and candy that is all or mostly chocolate.

In this heat I could feel the small miniature candy bars I had were soft, and I wasn't going to eat any knowing it would be messy. Unfortunately I couldn't resist and when I delicately opened one, the chocolate looks like soft butter that's stuck to the wrapper. So I lick it off. Then have a few more.

As I use a moist towelette to clean the sticky goo from my fingers, I'm pondering the conundrum over what gear is necessary and what isn't. What each biker decides to carry is highly personal and generally a balance between comfort and necessity, but there are fanatics who try to pare their gear to the bare minimum. At times I've wondered what it would be like to ride with a much lighter load, mostly when engaged in a climb that's going to last more than a few hours. Certainly moist towelettes would not be part of my gear. And I might be wearing the same clothes every day for 2 weeks or more and I'd be sleeping under a flimsy plastic tarp without protection from mosquitoes. Is it worth it? I could argue that if the three of us carried only the utter necessities, we might drop 10 pounds or more, each, and we could cover more miles with the same amount of energy. We might even bike a 100 miles a day on occasion, and there is certainly an advantage in that. But excuse me, we're talking about The Elite. If our gear weighed 10 pounds less we would most likely spend more time sitting on the side of the road eating candy or in a restaurant eating pie and drinking coffee, not biking more miles. And considering this, the sacrifice isn't worth it.

Most of the route had been fairly remote and we were used to riding with few cars on the road. We would often bike side by side and talk as we kept an eye on the rearview mirror. This comes to an abrupt end as we get close to Whitefish. Traffic picks up, the shoulder shrinks and cars zip by as we hug the white line at the edge of the road. As if this isn't bad enough, there are also some tough, short climbs that slow us down just as we are trying to rush through the congestion, and it's still quite hot. Anxiety builds as this goes on for a while until we finally approach the city.

Once we make it to the downtown area we leave the traffic behind, find a nice place for dinner, and pull out the maps to chart our progress. We're thinking of spending the night at the nearby Whitefish Lake State Park but we've only covered 60 miles so far.

Mark dives in and starts making calculations. I look up the date, check my train reservations and see that we have potentially 3 full days of riding left. I casually look at the map and try to compare the distance we've covered with what's left and there seems to be enough time.

"How does it look?" I ask Mark.

"Good. We'll make it into Glacier tomorrow, the next day over the pass, then the last day will be a short one for you, and Gary and I will head to Cut Bank, which is about three to four hours further after we split. We should be there by late afternoon or early evening."

"So it's going to be two long days?"

"No, two short days. Riding over the pass in Glacier will take some time, though it will be shorter on miles than our average."

"What? I thought we were behind schedule?"

"I thought we had to make up more miles too but unless I'm reading the map wrong, we should have plenty of time.

"Huh, all this anxiety about making our destination on time and we're actually ahead of schedule."

"Well, yesterday was a long day and there were a few others when we did more than our average."

"Right. I just thought with the detour we must be further behind."

"Apparently not. Tomorrow is going to be a short day mainly because of the restriction on the Going To The Sun Road, but that's not a problem."

"Oh yeah, I forgot about that. So we'll stay here tonight."

"Sounds good."

After dinner we head off-route about two miles to the campground at Whitefish Lake State Park. There we find sites that are well maintained and widely spaced with a lot of big trees. At some campgrounds you're crammed in like a suburban house in a subdivision, all trees removed as if they're a nuisance. I always wonder if there is anyone who actually likes camping in those kind of places.

During the last few moments of daylight I scribble some notes in my journal. There isn't much activity in the campground and everything is quiet and still. When it's too dark to write I crawl into the tent, plop down on the foam pad and pull the sleeping bag around my neck. I frequently feel I'll lay awake for hours because it's always much earlier than I normally go to bed, but without fail, barely 10 minutes pass before I'm out.

As we packed up the next day, there was no hurry to start riding. We have a leisurely breakfast, then decide to do laundry. I'm almost out of money so I reluctantly take a cash advance against my credit card not because it's the best option, but the only one I have. I just don't want to be in a situation where I need cash and don't have any.

Out of Whitefish we follow Highway 2 toward Columbia Falls. There is a lot more development and traffic than what we are used to, which is practically none, having come through some remote areas over the last couple of days. There are still wide patches of forest but comparatively, the congestion and development seem like such an annoyance.

We find a place for lunch and then a while later, in Columbia Falls, we see an ice cream stand. Finding it impossible to pass we decide on milkshakes for a change. It's been partly cloudy and warm this morning and we sit outside in a relaxed and laid back manner in no particular hurry to get to our destination.

From there we are routed north on a much less traveled road and it's good to get away from some of the congestion. Eventually the road will curve east and we'll be heading toward Glacier National Park.

The clouds move on and the sun is brilliant. It's hot and we're sweating. The road takes us into a more remote area and we come to a gravel section, which is not a surprise because it's labeled on the map. The road is in relatively good condition but it's tougher riding than gliding along on pavement.

The temperature can't be that high but with all the cool weather we've encountered so far, it seems oppressive. I can feel the sweat on my face and my arms are glistening. Suddenly a car drives by and the dust hangs in the air coating my skin and irritating my nose. The gravel lasts about five miles, then it's a short ride into West Glacier, the town just outside the park, where we find a place for dinner.

As we leave West Glacier we get on a paved bike path that takes us into the park and the two miles to Apgar, at the southwest edge of the long and narrow Lake McDonald. This is where the campground and other services are. Our map warned about the availability of campsites inside the park during tourist season but there are quite a few that are empty, even now at the end of June.

We get a site and set up tents under a canopy of large trees.

We're pretty grimy so I turn to Gary and say, "Know what I'm thinking? Full body immersion! Can you can handle it this time?" I'm poking fun at Gary who used that phraseology on the first segment, then after Mark and I jumped in, decided not to.

"There aren't any showers around here, are there?"

"None."

We change and head down to a small boat launch where there is a dock.

"The water is going to be cold because the lake is fed by snowmelt. I can understand if you chicken out," I say to Gary as he walks out onto the dock.

"Go ahead, I'll take your picture." Gary dips his foot in. He turns his head and says, "Yep, it's cold," and lets out some nervous laughter. He stands on the edge for a moment shifting his weight back and forth then makes a nice dive off the end. Mark follows and I set my camera down then jump in feet first.

The cold water is a shock and when I surface, involuntarily blurt out, "Ugh!" then mockingly say, "Refreshing!" We laugh.

The lake is calm. Tall mountains, many of which still have snow on them, surrounded us. The park is quiet. A few campers stroll through the open, level area at the end of the lake. If the water was warmer I would be tempted to float around on my back, sit on the end of the dock for a while and plunge in again. But even with a little splashing around it wasn't long before a chill set in, and with the air temperature falling I jump out and wrap myself in a towel.

Back at camp we start a fire as it's getting dark. I reach into the pocket of my pannier and pull out a bag of small candy bars. "Chocolate anyone?"

The warm glow of the fire pushes back the cool air and the smokey aroma mixes with the scent of pine trees. It's a quiet, calm night. No one is camped close to us but we can see some of the other campers through the trees. Barely a peep is heard from anyone. As we stare into the fire Mark says, "Living the dream."

We tried to get an early start, really, but it wasn't much earlier than most. And that might be a problem because bicycles aren't allowed on the western half of the Going to the Sun Road between 11:00 am and 4:00 p.m. from Apgar Campground to Sprague Creek and from Logan Creek to Logan Pass. This is a safety issue, the road is narrow and in places potentially treacherous when vehicles and cyclists are trying to share it. The first restriction is the beginning of our route, so that's not a problem. It's the part that runs along Lake McDonald and is comparatively flat. The second is the last part of the climb and will come at the end of the road that leads to the pass, which ascends approximately 3000 feet in 30 miles. Climbing like this will dramatically reduce our speed but it's hard to tell how much time we'll need until we're actually doing it, so we're not sure when we'll get to the top.

To further add to this dilemma, the restaurant we had planned on getting breakfast from wasn't open when we were ready to ride, so there was a short delay before we could eat and depart.

The sun is low enough on the horizon when we leave that we're riding in the shade along the only flat section of the road. Soon we overtake a pair of bike tourers and adjust our pace so we can talk for a while. They're on the same route covering a shorter segment and traveling lighter, carrying less gear and staying in motels. We compare notes about our trips, and after a few minutes one of the bikers does a double take.

"Hey, I recognize your bikes," he says excitedly. "One day I saw them outside this restaurant and then about an hour later they were parked outside an ice cream shop!"

We all laugh hard. We have to admit we often have a difficult time passing up dessert or if it had been an hour or more since we last ate, an ice cream shop, coffee house or diner for some homemade pie. Therefore it's probably not surprising that none of us lose any weight on these trips, though we try to downplay this fact. Yes, it takes a special person to be a member of The Elite and this is another example that our moniker is anything other than serious.

There is barely any traffic and we casually ride side by side while we all continue to talk about the highlights of our trip and previous trips we've taken. The sun moves higher in the sky, the shadows shrink and it feels good when the light finally shines on us. When the grade steepens, the three of us dig in and leave our friends behind.

As we gain altitude the forest begins to clear and we're treated to magnificent views of the surrounding mountains. Tall, thin waterfalls crash onto the rock face, turn into thin rivers that meander around obstacles then fall again and bury themselves in the lush green landscape. There are quite a few pockets of snow in spite of the fact it's almost July. This is another area of the country that gets enough snow to bury the average house and combined with slides and avalanches this road is usually not clear until June.

In many places the road is narrow and decades ago, in order to prevent cars from riding off the edge, a stone wall was built along the side in many places. More recently the traditional guard rail has been added in a few other spots. It's a worthwhile precaution, in most places there is considerably drop off on the other side. The design and craftsmanship of the stone wall is quaint and comes from an era that's not likely to be repeated. But the wall, along with the guard rail, is short, maybe 2½ feet tall and if a cyclist were to haphazardly hit it, it seems he would easily fly over and fall to his death. Or that's what I keep envisioning, especially when a car crowds me to the edge.

This becomes more disconcerting as the climb doesn't relent, you become more tired, and hot, and you're gasping to catch your breath not just because you're steadily exerting yourself but also because the air is a bit thinner up here. It also doesn't help that traffic picks up considerably the later in the day it gets.

I'm torn between stopping every couple of hundred feet to take a photo of yet another impressive scene and pressing forward since it's getting late. In places where the road is a little wider, I can stop, place my right foot on the guard rail, keep my left hand on the brake to keep from rolling backward, and grab the camera for a quick shot.

It was a long, grueling ride and I'm pretty sure we violated the 11:00 rule but I don't know by how much. I'm happy to finally get to the top and jump off the bike without checking. We aren't sure what would have happened if caught by a park ranger and don't really want to think about it.

The first thing I notice at the pass are mountain goats and I grab my camera in search of a good photo. There is a large parking lot here and a big visitor center, which makes it a popular stopping point. The crowd is quite big and tourists race around as if they're on a tight schedule and afraid they might miss something.

Mark and Gary are taking a break while dark, heavy clouds move in. As I walk back toward them it starts to rain. We step inside the visitor center, look at some of the exhibits and wait for it to stop. The shower is short lived and I'm relishing some time off of the bike and want to hike around a bit. Gary decides to lay on a bench and Mark and I walk a ways down a trail. We don't have to go too far before we leave the buzz and bustle of the crowd behind. We hike over some snow and through tall brush and trees and enjoy the expansive view. It starts to lightly rain so Mark turns around and heads back. I flip up my hood and go on, hoping for some good photos but about 15 minutes later I head back too.

The rain is light but steady and as we're getting ready to leave we see our bike touring friends. We ride over.

"How's it going?"

"We were busted."

"What?"

"It was after 11:00 and we were still riding. A ranger caught us. He told us we'd have to stop and sit on the side of the road until someone gave us a ride."

"Who was supposed to do that?"

"I don't know, but we stuck out our thumbs and a guy in a pickup brought us to the top. Maybe he felt sorry for us because he thought we couldn't make it."

The three of us start to laugh.

"What?"

"I'm pretty sure we didn't make it here before 11:00, so I guess we just got lucky," Gary says.

"How long did you have to wait before someone picked you up?" Mark asks.

"Not long. Everything worked out fine."

We wish our friends good luck, then head toward the end of the parking lot and check for traffic.

The road curves down and away. I cinch the drawstring on my hood and tilt my head down so the visor can deflect some of the oncoming rain as I take off. I grip the brake levers lightly to moderate my speed and prevent slipping on glossy turns. With the hood up it's hard to hear cars coming from behind and the rearview mirror doesn't help much as the road twists and turns, so I ride to the side and cars give me a wide berth.

The descent goes on for a long time. At a few points I stop and pull off the road to take some photos. In one, I frame up Gary from a distance where the road doubles back with a tall mountain behind him to show the magnitude of our surroundings. He zips by and I continue riding.

The curves aren't as tight on this side of the mountain and the shoulders are wider so it's easy to see why there aren't any restrictions here.

It seems like the rain is letting up as the road levels out but as we're leaving the park it comes down quite hard. Gary points to a restaurant off to the right and we gladly follow him inside.

After dinner the rain stops but the clouds refuse to move on. We bike up the road and find a campground. Rain threatens, but holds off as we set up and settle in.

Tomorrow is the last day of this segment. We'll all ride south for 20 miles then split at the 49/89 junction. I'll head south for another 10 miles to the town of East Glacier and catch the train the next morning. Gary and Mark will head east another 42 miles to the town of Cut Bank. From there they'll rent a truck and drive south to Great

Falls to catch a flight the next day.

In the morning we break camp, find a place to eat and head south. It's a little bit of a let down that the trip is ending, but after two weeks of steady riding I'm ready for a break if nothing else. It's still early in the day when we arrive at the junction and after brief parting hand-shakes and wishes of good luck I continue south to East Glacier as Gary and Mark head east toward Cut Bank.

Once in town, I ask around and find a campground that is basically a field behind a building where I'm the only occupant. There is a bath-room with showers so I have everything I need and don't mind being alone. I set up and make a mental list of the things I have to do.

First, I ask where the post office is and go get the package I had mailed to myself from Seattle. Next, I find the train station to make sure I know how to get there tomorrow. The station is a large, log cabin structure that has a small office and waiting area that's only open when the train is in town, but also a covered outside area. When you stand on the platform you half expect to see an old steam-driven locomotive pull up. I take a few photos and then explore the small town a bit. I find a restaurant that looks good for dinner, a small number of nondescript businesses and a Laundromat. I wasn't going to do laundry but realize everything I have is dirty and besides, I have plenty of time to do it. I also find a grocery store where I buy some candy and snacks for the train, and a restaurant for breakfast within walking distance of camp.

After dinner I start to pack everything up. Things that I won't need anymore go into the box. I have a small duffle for the train and all of those items go in there. The train is scheduled to leave at 10:30 a.m. and I need to get there early, buy a box for my bike, tear it down a bit and pack it up.

Everything seems under control so I get out one of the paperbacks I brought for the train and read until dark.

At the crack of dawn I wake to faint light and heavy rain. "Great," I say out loud, then roll over and go back to sleep. It's after 8:00 when I wake for good and it's still raining hard. I put on my rain gear and walk to the restaurant. It won't take longer than half an hour to get to the train station and pack up my bike but I don't want to cut it too close. The rain continues through breakfast and a few more cups of coffee as I read my book. It's still raining hard when I walk back.

I pack up everything in the tent, put the blue box outside, the cardboard box on top of it, my duffle on top of that and a large plastic bag that I cut flat to use as a small tarp. The tent comes down and is stuffed into the blue box along with a pint of water. I attach the blue box to the bike and balancing the cardboard box on my handlebars covered with the piece of plastic, I ride to the train station with the duffle slung over my shoulder. I'm frustrated it's been raining hard for over two hours now and hope the cardboard box doesn't get so wet it'll break apart and I'll loose some of my stuff. The gravel road makes it difficult to steer and balance the box especially as I try to avoid large puddles.

Under the eave of the train station, I break down the bike to the extent that I need to, in order to fit it in the box, then tape it up. I wrap some tape around the lid and body of the blue box then check everything except the duffle I'll carry on the train.

I walk around to the covered platform where a few people are waiting. There is a couple sitting on a bench who are wearing rain pants that match their parkas and heavy hiking boots. I talk to them briefly and learn of their two week backpacking trip in the park where it rained nearly every day.

I look out toward the mountains. It's still raining and heavy clouds obscure the view. I think about the trip and how far we've come, almost halfway. The train crosses the plains not far from our route so I got a preview of what the next segment will be like. From here, the eastern edge of the Rockies, the terrain will flatten out, trees will all but vanish replaced by tall grass bobbing in the breeze, with a road that stretches straight ahead into the horizon. As far as geography goes, it will be a much different trip.

A few moments later I hear the rumble, then feel the vibration through the platform as the train shoots by and coasts to a stop.

Interlude

During the winter, the three of us make plans for the next segment across the plains. As the weather warms up, Mark and I learn Gary won't be riding with us on the next segment. We taunt him a bit about his decision but respect it. Mark and I are single and without children. Gary is married and now has a daughter, so he has a different set of priorities.

Mark and I agreed that biking during the longer days of late spring/ early summer was beneficial and plan the upcoming segment for the same time of year. We look at travel options to get back to East Glacier and taking the train makes the most sense, so we build a plan around that.

We also decide to carry the stove, fuel bottle, a pot, cups and spoons, just in case. There will be remote areas on our trip across the plains and we aren't sure if we'll need this stuff, but if we do, trying to buy these things on route might be difficult.

I continue to refine my gear. I liked the plastic box on top of my rear rack. It was waterproof and easier to put a jacket in or take one out than digging through my bags, which always seem stuffed to the brim. But the big blue box was too big, too heavy, and situated on my bike transversely, not very wind resistant. Though in all honesty, riding with it was less difficult than I thought it was going to be.

In trying to design some other options there are three large items that demand consideration: the sleeping bag, foam pad and tent. Gary offered Mark the use of his tent, so of the two tents I own, I have to decide which I'll use, and how much space that will take. I know that if I use a small box for the back I'll most likely need a front rack and bags. The solution I come up with uses a smaller plastic box for the top of my rear rack that can carry the foam pad and a few other items. Additionally, I make a rack and use wastebaskets in place of front panniers, with waterproof fabric covers for the top. The sleeping bag will go in one and the tent in the other. That way if the tent is wet it will be isolated. Again, I can't find a wastebasket the exact size I want but go with one that's a little big. Looking at the finished design in my garage before the trip, I don't feel like it's ideal, but I'm happy with what I came up with.

The decision to carry the bigger of the two tents was easy. The bigger one doesn't weigh that much more and it's easier to set up. The smaller one has a canopy that goes to the ground and is so dense it's like sleeping in a cave. I prefer the brighter one.

The pocket I added to my rear pannier worked so well I got some more fabric and a zipper, and built a new one for the other pannier.

As I pack everything up, I'm a lot more comfortable with the system I've worked out this time compared to the last segment.

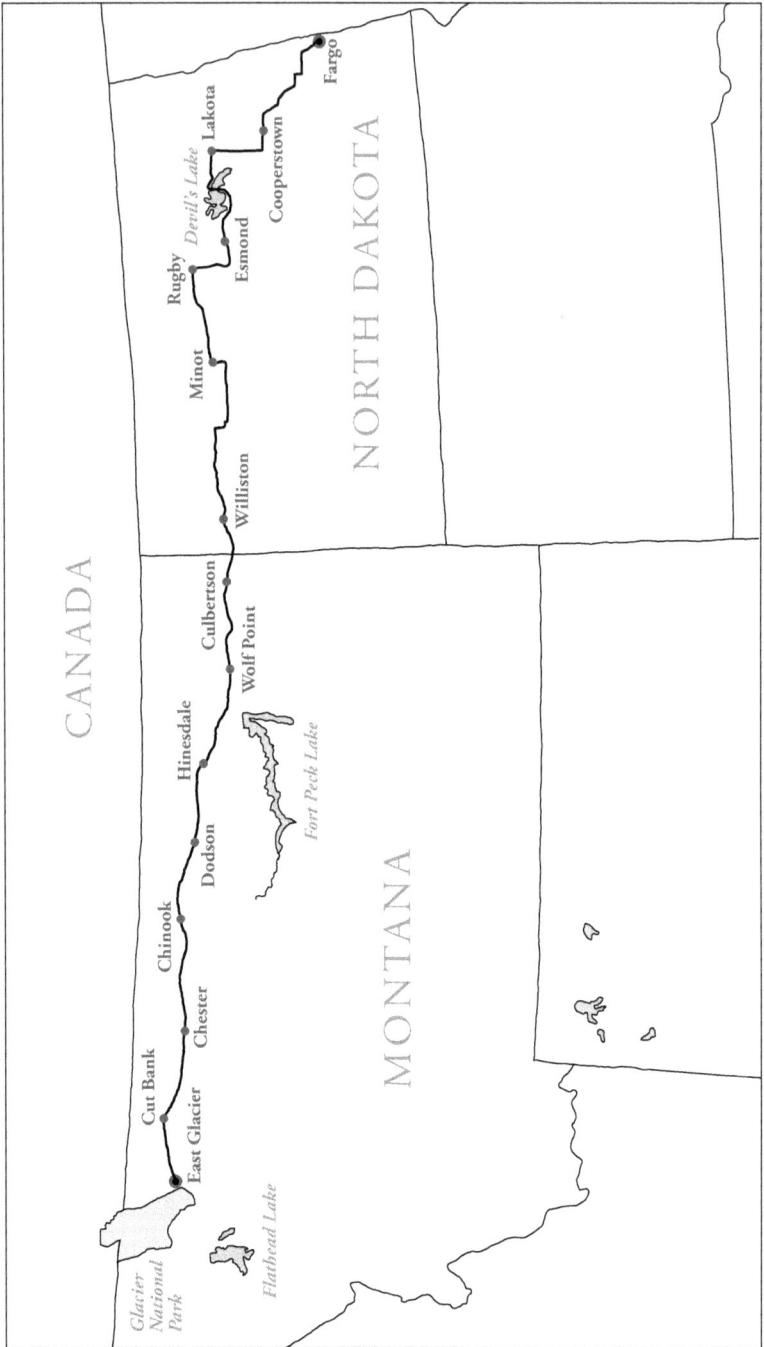

CANADA

NORTH DAKOTA

MONTANA

Glacier National Park

Flathead Lake

Fort Peck Lake

Devil's Lake

East Glacier
Cut Bank
Chester
Chinook
Dodson
Hinesdale
Wolf Point
Culbertson
Williston
Minot
Rugby
Esmond
Lakota
Cooperstown
Fargo

Plains

"Sure is windy," Mark says, as we look out the window of the train. We're both mesmerized as we watch small shrubs being whipped around as if they're caught in a tornado.

"Look at that," I say, pointing to a flag that's shredded and looks as if the wind is going to violently rip it off its pole. The train had come to a stop in a small town in central Montana. By bike, we're probably three or four days ride from East Glacier and realizing our fear that the wind would play havoc with us on this segment of the trip.

Mark and I decided to drive to Fargo, North Dakota, our destination, and take the train to East Glacier, Montana, the start of this segment. We could have taken the train from Detroit, but this way we wouldn't have to worry about meeting a specific deadline if something prevented us from finishing on time, or wait for the train if we finished early.

The Empire Builder is a group of trains that travel between Chicago, Illinois and Seattle, Washington. One leaves every day from Chicago for the two-day ride. It leaves at the same time every day so it arrives at the same time every day in Fargo, North Dakota. That time is 3:39 a.m.

Weary from the long drive, Mark and I unload the boxes that contain our bikes and gear. We haul them inside the small station. Not surprisingly, beside the station manager, we are the only ones here. We check our gear and Mark takes a seat, it'll be a little while before the train comes.

I walk outside with my camera. It's a still, warm night and everything is shut down and dark. I wander aimlessly through the parking lot and think about leaving Mark's truck here for the next two weeks but we're told it's alright. I step onto the tracks and look down into the night. Nothing but black. I turn back toward the station and see the profile of Mark's head framed in the window. Click.

I step back inside and sit opposite of Mark. We're talked out and sit in silence for the next 15 minutes until I feel the rumble of the train, then we gather our gear and go outside. The Empire Builder has two stories, like the buses you see on the streets of London and the seats are up top. We climb the narrow staircase and find two open seats next to each other, plop down and settle in. I check my ticket and we arrive at 6:45 this evening. 10 minutes later I'm asleep.

I wake a few times during the night. The lights are dim and everything is quiet. I nod out and wake for good at 10:30 am.

We're somewhere in North Dakota. It's cloudy and looks like rain. I try to reassure myself by thinking that weather generally moves from west to east and if we hit rain soon there's a good chance that it will pass by the time we get to our destination. Of course this isn't always true, but there is a big covered area at the station in East Glacier so we'll have a dry place to assemble the bikes and get ready to ride, rain or not.

The train isn't very full and at one of the stops enough passengers depart leaving plenty of empty seats. Mark moves across the aisle into one of two empty seats next to each other. I take my gear off the floor and place it in the seat next to me then angle my body and stretch out my legs.

A little later we take a trip to the lounge car for coffee, then check out the observation car where windows curve up into the ceiling. On the right side of the car the tall grass reaches out to the horizon and into the low hanging clouds. On the left side, a hundred yards away, a road runs parallel and I figure it's Highway 2, the road we'll be on for a good part of our trip. It starts to rain but we're hopeful it will be clear further west.

Back in our seats I'm paging through magazines that will be left behind when we reach our destination. On our way back from the observation car I stopped and got some more coffee and am now snacking on a something that is portraying itself as a moderately healthy, granola bar substitute but is actually a cookie in disguise. Not that I'm complaining much, it's good, and I follow it up with some peanut M&Ms. Later I break out the dried banana chips I brought.

We arrive in East Glacier according to schedule, get our gear and start to assemble the bikes. This is where I ended the last segment of our trip, just to the east of Glacier National Park, at the edge of the Rockies. It's clear and sunny, a little on the cool side but warm enough for shorts. The mountains can be seen just over the top of the trees and they are heavily coated with snow. I take a few photos of us assembling the bikes and when we're done, we ride up to the restaurant I ate at last year. Instead of camping we opt for a bunk in a small cabin with 4 other people, hostel-style accommodations. Outside the temperature has dropped considerably but inside the heat seems to be on full blast. After a few minutes I kick off the sleeping bag and fall asleep.

We discuss the day's plan over breakfast. The route on the touring map heads north after it leaves Glacier National Park, goes into Canada then loops around and comes back to the town of Cut Bank. Instead, we'll head directly toward Cut Bank and reconnect with the route, which then heads in an easterly direction. We figure we should be there for lunch.

It's cool and overcast as we set out. We quickly leave the cover of town and stands of trees behind. The landscape is opening up and slowly we can see further into the distance until trees and buildings disappear and the vast plain is exposed. We feel the breeze build until once in the open, with nothing to block it, the wind is voracious.

It's easy to see that the wind is strong but it's at our backs, pushing us along, which means the air around us is almost calm. It's only when we take our first break, the full impact of its strength is felt.

When we stop, we turn around, put our backs to it and lean forward, pushing against the balls of our feet. I parked my bike parallel to the wind out of fear that it would be pushed over if set broadside.

Our cloths ripple like an agitated flag fighting the grip of its pole and I squint to prevent dust and debris from flying into my eyes. If we are more than five feet from each other it is hard to hear without shouting.

I drink some water and look around. Behind us, the mountains are sinking into the horizon. To the side, rocky hills are the final remnants of this vast range. Ahead, the gently rolling landscape and nearly treeless plain spreads before us.

We get back on the bikes and the wind pushes us along. Unlike the last segment where we had to snake our way through an uneven topography, our route is mostly a direct shot through Montana. I can see the mountains in my rearview mirror. It will be the last time I see them on this trip and it's amazing how quickly the terrain is changing. The map indicated an elevation drop of 1000 feet or so as we ride toward Cut Bank and there are some long downhill sections that verify this. Between the terrain and wind we are devouring miles.

An hour or so later, Mark slows and steers to the side of the road for a break. After taking some water, I grab my camera and fire off of few shots. As we're ready to ride I peel off my wind shell to store it. Mark starts pedaling and I flip up the lid to my new plastic box. I had placed some Velcro on the ends to further secure it and could pop it open much like the trunk of a car. Holding the lid with one hand and stuffing the jacket inside with the other, I must have held it open just enough for the wind to get underneath.

In an instant the lid is violently ripped out of my hand and takes off like a rocket until it's high in the air, bobbing around like a kite and getting smaller by the second. As I stand there staring at it, I imagine riding for the next two weeks without a cover and try to think up some kind of make-shift lid, but I come up empty. This is not a good thing. I immediately steer my bike off the road and down into a gully that is 10 feet lower than the grade of the road, I don't want any of my other things blowing around. Then I take off in a sprint across the grassland. The lid is losing altitude and finally takes a nosedive into the ground, bounces up and turns into a tumbleweed rolling at great speed over the top of the grass. I envision myself running endlessly, the lid always just out of my reach, but then it stops. I finally catch up and am about 20 feet from it when it jumps like a giant frog, then a couple of more times before it rests and I'm able to pounce on it.

At some point Mark realized I wasn't behind him, turned around and came back to find me. As I walk up to my bike with the lid under my arm Mark shouts, "What happened?" I hold up the lid with both hands firmly grasping it, "I lost it."

I snap it back in place, push my bike up onto the road and explain to Mark what happened. "How far did the wind take it?"

"Um…" I look out over the swaying grass, "maybe 250 yards or more."

Mark starts laughing, no doubt visualizing me running like a maniac after the cover. And now that I had secured the lid, I was laughing too.

Early in the afternoon it starts to rain and we stop in Cut Bank for lunch while trying to avoid some of it. Luckily, the rain is light and only lasts about an hour. It isn't long after when the clouds break, the sky clears and the sun comes out.

We are giddy having the wind as our ally. With minimal effort we maintain speeds in the low 20s while hauling 40 pounds or more of gear. I sit upright and try to steer without my hands, exposing my entire back to the wind to give it something to push against but my skill seems to be lacking and I quickly grasp the handlebars again. After a few more tries I give up considering there doesn't seem to be a difference in my speed and I really don't want to crash. Traffic is very light, which isn't surprising since we've only passed through a couple of small towns. The road is in good condition and we sail along with ease.

The sun is shining, the temperature is warm, and it feels good to be on the bike and riding, near effortlessly. The wind is voracious and at our backs. It's like a dream.

We stop for dinner in Shelby and after a nice break we're ready to ride again. The sun casts long, angled shadows of us as we zip along with ease.

By the time we set up camp in Chester, we covered 118 miles, the longest single day mileage so far on the trip. Knowing that our average is around 63 and our longest day so far is 87, it looks like this is going to be a high point that will be hard to beat. Still, it's the first day and we usually grow stronger as trip progresses, though it would be hard to imagine the wind could blow much harder without tornado warnings.

The next day we wake to sunny skies and have a somewhat leisurely attitude toward breaking camp. We can afford to be lazy, we have essentially covered two days worth of riding in one.

After we break camp I'm ready to ride, straddling my bike, waiting for Mark. He loads his panniers, then stands by his bike combing his hair. I didn't even bring a comb. I poke fun at Mark, "I don't know why you're wasting your time trying to make yourself look good, it's a lost cause. Hot chicks aren't even going to give you the time of day."

Mark smiles, then trying to sound philosophical, says, "Did you ever hear the joke about the two guys in the woods who see a bear?"

"Ah... refresh my memory."

"There are two guys in the woods and they're setting up camp when all of a sudden they see a bear. One of the guys grabs his shoes and starts to put them on and the other says, 'Why are you putting on your shoes, you can't outrun a bear?' The first guy says, 'I don't have to outrun the bear, all I have to do is outrun you!'" Mark then adds, "I don't have to look good, I only have to look better than you!"

We laugh and I say, "Ok, ok, clever boy, just get on your bike and ride."

A few miles down the road we find a diner for breakfast. As we are walking in I notice a small hand-written note on the door. The note says, "It's Mary's birthday today, come in and wish her a happy birthday." It's the kind of thing you see in small towns where everybody knows one another. We sit down and a very nice, gorgeous young woman waits on us. When we finish ordering, I ask if her name is Mary. Looking perplexed she says, "Yes," and I say "Well, happy birthday Mary."

Mary starts gushing, "Awwww, that is so nice. Thank you, you are sooo nice. That was really special." She then walks away and I lean toward Mark and say, "Don't worry, I'm sure your hair made a good first impression."

After breakfast we get back on Highway 2. The air is cool and while I ride in shorts, I still wear a wind jacket over my t-shirt. I'm a little stiff from yesterday's mileage but otherwise feel good.

The wind is more sporadic and certainly not as strong but still helpful. At this point we're quite happy having the wind as our ally, and since we're riding from west to east, which is the way the prevailing wind blows, we anticipate a pleasant and leisurely ride over the next two weeks.

I can tell I'm carrying a lot more weight than in the past. I have some fruit juice that was leftover from the train and a lot more snacks than I need, though I figure this stuff will be gone soon enough. I decided to take the bigger of the two tents I own and am carrying all the weight instead of splitting it with Mark because he's borrowing Gary's tent. I have a couple of extra items of clothing and as light a tripod as I could find which still weighs close to two pounds. The new plastic box I have is smaller and weighs less than the old one but I also have two new front panniers made of wastebaskets, and a frame to connect them to the bike, and the result is a weight gain over last year. I was a bit reckless this time since over the previous two segments I became used to the weight I was carrying and knew we wouldn't be climbing like we had done in the past, but I should have been more judicious because I can tell the difference.

Our pace is slower and for a while the sky is overcast but becomes sunny again. There aren't many places for lunch so we snack at breaks throughout the afternoon. Havre looks like a good spot for dinner and we stop, then bike 22 miles further to Chinook to camp.

It was another long day and we topped 85 miles. At this rate we might end the trip three or four days early. Once we're used to riding with the weight of our gear, we might consistently do 100 miles a day. Compared to the last segment, where we were constantly climbing and wriggling our way through the mountains, it seems like we're making progress by leaps and bounds.

After I take a shower, I look in the mirror and am surprised to see how red my face is, it didn't seem like it had been that sunny so far. I have a large pair of sunglasses so I'm starting to look like a raccoon. A raccoon with four-day stubble. And uncombed hair.

Getting ready to leave the next morning, it seems as if the wind has picked up considerably. Once we get back on route we realize our happy dream has ended. Not by a little or gradually, but abruptly and harshly. The wind has shifted nearly 180 degrees and it's the same strong, vehement force that had made our first day so enjoyable. Now, coming almost straight at us, we are miserable from nearly the moment we leave camp. During the first couple of hours I keep thinking the wind might taper off or change directions to a degree that would make it easier on us, but I always come back to the first day when it blew at our backs so hard for the entire day without letting up.

If this isn't the most grueling biking I have ever encountered, then it's certainly near the top of the list. It's a dogfight every inch of the way as we struggle to maintain seven mph. There is no coasting. The wind is strong enough to stop us even on gentle downhill sections of the road without pedaling. Mark and I try to suck it up the best we can but there is much grimacing, swearing, and frustration.

We are heading almost directly east but the road twists and turns enough so it seems like the wind is seldom right in front of us, which renders drafting useless. It's an odd thing, fighting this entity we can't see, even though we can perceive the effects of its existence. Grass bends and bobs. Trees sway and creak. Tumbleweeds zip by. Dust and debris fly through the air. My shirt ripples, the bike twists, the resistance is maddening.

It had been partly cloudy with intermittent sunshine but because it's so windy it's hard to tell how hot it is. Making forward progress has been extremely strenuous but any amount of sweat I'm producing is quickly carried away by the wind. We arrive in Harlem around noon and I see a lighted sign on a building that says it's 75 degrees. It could be much warmer and we're thankful it's not.

As we move forward, I'm hunkered down, gripping the drop handlebars, and trying to make myself as wind resistant as possible. And this goes on for hours. There is nothing pleasant about it.

Mid afternoon we come to a hilly area covered with a stand of trees. I stop to take a break and hike off the road and down into the trees about 30 feet. The roar of the wind with its invisible force that constantly pushes at us, dissipates. Mark follows and sits on the ground a couple of yards away. "I had to get out of the wind."

"I don't blame you."

I smile, "It's nice to be able to talk without shouting."

"Yeah, and hear without the roar of the wind rushing across your ears."

We sit in silence, almost too tired to talk, both of us slumped over.

Finally, Mark says, "I looked at the map and I don't think we're going to make it to the next campsite. At the rate we're going it's just too far away."

"Well, if we have to camp on the side of the road there are plenty of spots to pitch a tent. Hopefully we can find someplace with trees to block the wind."

Eventually we pull ourselves up, climb back toward the road, get on the bikes, and prepare to fight our way forward. As we inch ahead I shout to Mark, "We're living the dream!" It roused a smile, but at this point there isn't much to laugh about, as we stand on the pedals, tense our muscles and start to dig in, while the bikes slowly creep forward.

A few more hours down the road, it's getting late and far from a campground we find a bar where we can get dinner on the outskirts of Dodson. Dead tired, we sit at a table and order. A small group of cowboys are sitting at the bar looking over at us and giggling to themselves. "Hey," I say to Mark, motioning with my chin, "those guys over there are laughing at the black girdle you're wearing. Obviously they don't know we are part of The Elite. You should go kick their butt."

Without looking Mark smiles, "I'd do it but I'm too tired to even get up and walk over there. Hey, why don't you do it for me?" I smile, too tired to think of a witty comeback.

After dinner we scan the horizon and consider setting up the tents in a field when I remember I saw an old sign for a bed and breakfast as we rode up to the bar, about 30 yards back. The sign is in a condition that made me think the place was long gone, but it's worth a shot. After a short ride to grab the phone number and a quick call, we gladly opt for a hot shower and sanctuary from the wind.

We're shown to a room that looks like it had just been remodeled. It's neat, clean and nearly everything seems new. Whenever we're a bed short we take turns sleeping on the floor. In this room there is only one double bed.

"I can't remember whose turn it is to sleep on the floor."

"Me either, but I was thinking it's not much of a sacrifice to sleep on this," Mark says as he looks down. "The carpet looks brand new and the pad under it seems like it's an inch thick. Well, it's your call."

It didn't matter much to me, the next time we'd switch. "I'll take the bed."

I set my stuff on the bed and sit down on the edge, glad to be inside. The wind, though muffled now, roars. It rustles the trees and pushes against the sides of the house with great force, making it creak and moan. It's surprising how exhausting a hard wind is. Simply standing becomes a chore, you have to exert yourself just to stay upright.

We covered about 50 miles in roughly seven hours of riding. If we run into more days like this it's going to take us a long time to get to Fargo and it isn't going to be an enjoyable trip. So far the wind has either pushed us along or fought against us. In the end it might balance out, but I don't know if I'm willing to fight as hard as I did today if the wind is this nasty again.

It's a little too early in the trip to be jumping to conclusions or trying to predict what might happen. I force myself up and into the shower. When my head hits the pillow I'm dead to the world.

Just as it's turning light, I can hear rain beating against the window.
"Are you awake?"
"Yeah."
"It's raining."
"Yeah."
"So now we have to fight the wind and the rain?"
"We could stay in bed all day."
"Yeah."
We doze for a while longer but the rain continues through breakfast and while packing up. Raingear-clad, we attach our bags to the bikes and realize the wind has died down considerably. After the fierce headwind yesterday it's a welcome, but not pleasant, trade off.

We set off at a relatively slow pace. My hood is up with the helmet over that, while rain sprays my face and soaks my shoes. It's a dull, dark day. The wind whips around in bursts, almost in a circular pattern. It's as if it's poking at us, toying with us. We trudge along, single file, without talking.

A few hours later and barely more than 20 miles up the road we stop for lunch, mainly to take a break from the weather. The rain has been incessant. I peel off my clammy rain jacket. I have shorts on under my rain pants but not wanting to pull the pants off over my wet and dirty shoes I pushed them down past my knees and plop down into a booth. This may look odd to the other patrons but I'm too soggy to care.

We're hoping that a leisurely lunch might give the rain an opportunity to pass over us but it's one of those days where it just doesn't let up. When we're finished, we secure our rain gear and step outside to the sound of raindrops splattering against our jackets and off the pavement, the cool damp air, the dark gray day. As we walk up to the bikes, Mark says, "Living the dream," in a deadpan manner and I can't help but smile.

Later in the afternoon, without much discussion, we bypass a scenic detour that includes a dirt road for 10 miles, figuring it would be muddy and difficult riding. The route would have taken us closer to Lake Bowdoin and the National Wildlife Refuge. This is the second challenging day in a row and we aren't inclined to make it any more difficult than necessary.

The landscape is dull and gray above the green, grassy prairie. The rain softens everything and blurs distant objects. Occasionally a car rushes by, headlights on, wipers flapping, the whoosh of wet pavement trailing off as it passes.

As the afternoon wears on the rain diminishes to a light haze and the wind kicks up a bit from the south creating a mild crosswind that becomes a nuisance. Still, we seem to be adjusting to the conditions and pick up our pace a bit. For dinner we stop in Saco and after a warm and dry break, bike another 15 miles to Hindsdale to camp.

We stop at the seemingly abandoned city campground. There are no facilities beside a pit toilet and the grass is two feet tall or higher everywhere. Though it's still gloomy and overcast it hasn't rained in a while. I set my gear on a picnic table at one of the sites, then trample the grass so I have a place to pitch the tent. The wind has picked up considerably and is now quite vicious even though we have some cover from widely spaced trees and brush that surround the area. I stake down the floor of the tent and run rope from the sides to the picnic table, a tree and the ground. My tiny fabric shelter twists and bends with large gusts that hit like waves. The tent strains and resists then violently shakes and shudders. It's amazing how loud it is. This goes on for most of the night along with heavy rain and wakes me from a deep sleep more than once.

In the morning the air is much calmer. The grass droops over after having been battered through the night and everything is soaked. We pack wet gear with rain threatening and can't find anywhere to get food except a gas station that has coffee and things like prepackaged muffins and doughnuts. We set off under cloudy skies avoiding puddles and hoping it will clear. Once we get back on Highway 2, a slight tailwind helps push us along.

Our route continues to take us through small towns, across farms so large they would perish without modern technology, and the wide-open vistas that characterize the prairie. While it's easy to associate Montana with mountainous terrain, most of the state is distinguished by sprawling clear spaces and rolling hills, like the other states of the plains.

We stop around noon for lunch in Glasgow but when I look at the menu decide to order breakfast instead. While it had been cloudy the entire morning we remained dry, but just as our food is served it starts to rain. We take our time eating and get a few more refills of coffee. Luckily, our stalling tactic works and it stops by the time we are ready to leave. Low, thick clouds still dominate the sky so we pull out our damp rain gear and put it on, then head toward the highway.

Barely 15 minutes out of town Mark unexpectedly pulls off the road. I ride up to the side of him, "What's wrong?"

"I have a flat."

It's easier to pull the wheel apart and put in a new tube rather than try to patch it right away, we can do that later in camp. We're both carrying spare tubes and have fixed plenty of flats so this isn't a big deal.

"Hey, maybe you need to replace that tire with the one you're carry-ing," I say making fun of the idea that the spare is necessary.

Mark chuckles, "You're going to be real sorry if you're ever stranded and need that tire."

Mark is an engineer, I'm not, so I add, "Maybe I'll just have to use my engineering prowess to come up with a better idea than carrying an extra tire across the country, *if* that ever happens."

"Or maybe you're going to be stranded on the side of the road!" We both laugh.

Another half hour down the road, we stop and pack the raingear. An hour later it starts to clear. Eventually we feel the warm rays of the sun and see vast blue skies. A gentle breeze caresses tall stalks of grass as it flows across the fields. The air is comforting, like a warm bath. Ahead, the two-lane highway stretches out to the horizon, black asphalt now faded gray, with lush, green grassy plains extending out from each side.

It's nice to be riding without excessive climbing and the zigzagging back and forth as the road makes it way through mountain passes. At the end of the day it seems like we've made real progress. Miles covered can be seen on a map and are not swallowed by the constant ascent and descent of vertical travel.

We fall into a steady rhythm and gliding along without a specific destination or the worry of falling behind schedule it's as if we're wandering aimlessly across a vast landscape. When we come into Wolf Point we had biked 88 miles, which is surprising.

The restaurant we pick has old-fashioned phones on each table and when you decide what you want to eat, you place your order by phone. There doesn't seem to be any practical advantage to this system but it's a unique curiosity. Once again, I order beef. We had passed numerous farms and though I didn't see any livestock aside from the occasional horse, I was under the impression a great steak or a fresh, superior cut of beef could be found at any restaurant. So far I had been disappointed. It's not that anything I had up to that point was bad, but nothing had been above average.

We order and eat. Our food is good, but I think I just confirmed this isn't cattle country.

A campground near town is home for the night. We pitch the tents and are eventually bathed in the golden glow of the last rays of the day as the sun touches the horizon. We talk a little of the weather and how the trip is going so far. Mark patches his tube then retires to write postcards. I enjoy the last moments of the day: the emerging sound of crickets, the fiery glow of endless tall grass, the faint cool breeze that barely ripples the smooth tent canopy, shadows eight times longer than the things they represent, the still calm of the approaching night.

At breakfast, I once again voice a weak complaint to Mark about the coffee. I enjoy a moderately strong brew but the preference of this region must be mild because I haven't been able to find anything to suit my taste since the start of the trip. It's a minor quibble and I know that if I bring it up often enough we'll be able to turn it into a joke.

We look over the route and talk about the availability of campgrounds. There is one 60 miles away and one after that, 97 miles away. We decide to see how long it will take to get to the closer one and take it from there. It's sunny and warm with a light tailwind. We figure we'll get to the closer one by late afternoon.

What starts the day as a benefit, the tailwind, only lasts about an hour or so. Slowly, it turns around and becomes a moderate headwind. When I begin to notice this, I check the map to see if the road had veered north or south to explain the shift, but we're still riding in a mostly eastern direction. Eventually a light wind that was pushing us along, has turned strong and is facing us. Up to this point the wind seemed to be fairly consistent. If it started the day in one direction then we could count on it to continue that way all day. It seems odd that it would change so dramatically in a matter of hours. We're frustrated by it's unpredictability, especially in this case since it's fighting us.

It seems as if the wind is either our ally or enemy. When working against us, it's easy to think we would gladly give up the joyous moments of tailwinds for no wind at all on the rest of this trip. I had noticed that the motto on the Montana license plate is, Big Sky, but after many unfavorable encounters with the wind I suggest to Mark they change it to, It Blows.

The headwind isn't as bad as it was a few days ago but bad enough to impede our forward progress and take the joy out of the ride. To add to the headwind, we also experience some rather steep hills, the first climbing we've encountered since we left East Glacier. I downshift once, twice, then bottom it out and push hard on the pedals, lowering my stance to the drop handlebars.

Mid afternoon we stop at a convenience store in a small town for a cold drink. I'm sitting outside when Mark comes out with a medium size bag.

"What do you have in there? Twinkies? Apple Pie? Donuts?" Mark laughs. "I saw some Ho Hos that had your name all over them. I would have bought them for you if I knew you were short."

"I was going to get that imitation cheese flavored popcorn for you." We laugh.

"I'll tell you what, if you have a good cup of coffee and a homemade brownie in there for me, I'll buy you dinner."

"No luck. How about a chocolate Pop Tart?"

"Works for me."

During breakfast we thought we would end up in Culbertson in the late afternoon since we'd be covering about 60 miles. So far, barring a strong headwind or all day rain we had managed to ride considerably more miles than that each day. Now, however, it isn't until early evening when we ride into town and find a place for dinner.

The waitress sees us pull up and after we're seated she walks over and asks about our trip. We engage in a friendly conversation recounting the notable features: the strong wind, the frequent rain, the difference between our lush home state and the vast prairie. She asks if we are spending the night and when we say yes, she tells us about a rodeo and gives us directions.

We find the campground, set up, and take showers. I never keep close track of time and I don't know if Mark does either. I check the time on occasion, but it just doesn't have much relevance and I'm happy to be without a specific schedule. It's still light and remembering it's Saturday, figure the festivities will go on for a while so we don't feel rushed.

We leave camp and riding without the weight of the gear on my bike is exhilarating. Mark takes off at a good clip and it seems like we can accelerate at a break neck speed and zip along with ease. My bike feels nimble and responsive, like a Ferrari rather than a freight train.

When we arrive at the small stadium it's twilight and the rodeo had just finished. Thinking there might be some other events, we're surprised when everyone slowly walks to their cars and leaves. By the time we head back it's dark and when we get to our campsite we call it a night.

Thunder and heavy winds wake me. It's dark. I reach for my electronic speedometer, the only device I have that tells the time and see that it's 2:00 a.m. I set it down and roll over. Then the lightening comes. The tent is swaying and twisting. The wind roars and suddenly the tent bends violently in one direction then pops back, is battered, shudders then is still for a moment. The low tremor of thunder builds to a blast and lightening turns night to day for a fraction of a second. This happens over and over while the wind makes the tent dance to a violent, erratic number.

I lay there and calculate the odds of being struck by lightening in this situation. I figure not so much and wonder where we'd go if there was imminent danger. I am awake for quite a while enjoying the show until I drift off.

It's light, but very dim and raining hard. It has to be early morning and I'm glad it's not time to get up or break camp. The muffled roar is soothing, especially since I'm warm and dry. I prop myself up on one arm and make a sweep of the tent where the walls meet the floor to see if any rain has leaked in and it's dry. I roll over, knowing I can sleep for a couple more hours and pull the sleeping bag tight around my neck.

This time as I come out of the haze of sleep, it's just after 9:00. I can hear light rain hit the tent. It's time to pack up and I grab the small things and put them in their respective pockets on the panniers. It's good to have some kind of system for where each item is stored so you don't have to waste time searching when you need something. Rain gear is pulled out, the sleeping bag rolled up along with the foam pad and put away. The rain covers for the panniers come out and are put in place. I pull on the rain pants, then put on my shoes, then my jacket, zip it up part way then flip up the hood. I unzip the door and step outside.

It has stopped raining! What a stroke of good luck.

Everything is saturated. The tent sags, the grass is squishy, there are big puddles everywhere. It's dark and gray. I roll the bike over and grab my bags and put them on the rear rack, then the plastic box on top and the sleeping bag in one of the front baskets. As the tent comes down I shake off as much water as I can and delicately fold it up. It goes into the other basket. At the same time Mark is following a similar procedure. I put the handlebar box in place and snap my electronic speedometer in its holder.

A few minutes later Mark looks over, "Ready?"

"I was born ready."

We jump on the bikes and start to pedal. I pull up next to Mark and he says, "Is that the motto of The Elite?"

"Either that, or, Will stop for food." We both laugh as we make our way back to the main part of town in search of breakfast.

It's dark and gloomy through the morning but we didn't get rained on. In the early afternoon it clears a bit and the dark blue-gray clouds that clustered near the horizon move on. It's still thick and gray overhead.

We stop for a break and dig through our bags for some food. We are on a ridge with the prairie spreading out below us. It's a vantage point where we can see far off into the distance. I look out at a small group of buildings scattered between a few clusters of trees almost a half mile away. It's darker over there and just inside of an area that is maybe a few hundred yards across, there are thick, low clouds and a torrent of rain. It's fascinating. I can see, as if from the outside, an entire rainstorm. It's like looking at a microcosm, a little world unto itself, as if it's separate from the world I'm living in. I stare for what is probably a short period of time but am so absorbed it seems much longer. I imagine those who live there scrambling to avoid getting wet and wonder if they can look out and see, that not far from where they are, it is perfectly dry.

Later in the afternoon we cross the state line and ride into North Dakota without fanfare. The only indication is a small sign on the immense prairie welcoming us. We steer off of the road and gravity pulls us through the tall grass to get near the sign. I set my camera on the tripod so I can snap a photo of both of us as we stand next to our bikes in knee-high grass.

A little ways down the road we encounter construction and roll over some sections of gravel while trying not to breath in plumes of dust from passing cars. It goes on for a few miles but it's Sunday so no one is working and there aren't any delays.

In the early evening we ride into Williston and find a place to eat. It's been mostly cloudy all day and at times it looked like we were going to get rained on but we've been lucky so far. Now the clouds are moving on and we're getting sunshine. There is a campsite near town and another about 15 miles down the road. After a nice break and a full stomach we decide to ride. The sun is out but the trade off is a brisk crosswind.

Before we reach camp, we encounter a series of steep hills that are the most challenging terrain up to this point. Surprisingly, if we had come on this during the west segment it would have seemed like a minor blip but after miles of level or gently rolling asphalt I feel like this is not just inconvenient, but an irritating nuisance. I was ready for a leisurely ride to wind down the day, but now I've dropped into the lowest gear, our pace slows and we're struggling to reach our pre-determined destination. As the steep hills continue, it feels like we've done more climbing in the last few miles than the entire trip. When concern grows about making it to the campground before dark and it seems like it's going to be an issue, we arrive at Lewis and Clark State Park.

On the edge of Lake Sakakawea, we set up in a near-vacant campground on lush grass under large trees. The facilities appear new, or recently remodeled and are spotless. We are quite impressed because not all of the places we've stayed at were first rate. Often, when it came time to camp, there was only one campground in the vicinity and the next one might be hours of riding away, so we'd have to settle for whatever we could find.

Many times we camped on patchy, dried out grass or dirt, but here the grass is nice carpet of soft green so I take off my shoes and socks and pitch the tent in bare feet. Our campsite is near the lake and when everything is set I walk the shore as small waves lap up and the sky turns shades of pink and dark blue.

There are concessions in the park but they're not open for the season yet and there isn't a town close by so we have to go quite a ways to get breakfast, but now used to the weight of the gear and the long days, gliding across the road in a consistent and rhythmic manner is a pleasure.

Riding across the prairie is like being in the middle of the ocean. There's an awesome vastness that you can't experience in the city, or the mountains, or anywhere that has an abundance of trees. Although you know it, acknowledging that the sky extends from straight out in front of you to, 180 degrees overhead, straight behind you, is humbling. Realizing that your world is dominated by sky, and the part you inhabit is a thin plain seems disconcerting. Yet the change from my normal life, the life I live day to day, is welcome. Gone are the regular routines, the schedules, the deadlines, the chaos. It's entirely appropriate that my experience of the physical world is different too.

It was hazy when we started this morning but quickly cleared and we are enjoying the sunny, warm weather. The terrain is hilly but the climbs are gentle and easy, and unlike the steep descents in the mountains that are quickly over, there is plenty of time to coast and recover on the backside.

As we float across the plain, my mind wanders without holding a thought. I've forgotten my other life temporarily, the demands and concerns, the responsibilities and issues. Physically, there is a near effortlessness that propels me and mentally I unburden myself with the things that drag me down.

Midday, after riding in silence for a while, Mark pulls up next to me and says "Sure is quiet without Gary here." We laugh.

I think about the previous segments when Gary was with us. A trip is defined not merely by the route but also by the personalities of the people who make up the group. Mark and Gary represent two opposites when it comes to conversation. Mark is generally quiet and measured, bordering on stoic at times. Gary is animated and frequently laughing, making jokes and taunting us, though he certainly doesn't have a patent on that, and is the most talkative. And while he could laugh it off, there did seem to be a number of little things that got under his skin.

I start to smile and say, "I sure do miss the litany of reasons why he didn't get a good night's sleep: Screaming drunken woman, street light shining like a beacon into his tent window, snorting deer..."

We laugh hard and Mark says, "Or how about the ever present problems with his bike: the bottom bracket, the constant adjusting of the handle bars. Oh, remember that mirror that he had on his helmet when we were out east? He had to adjust that thing about a 100 times a day... and he never liked that seat of his."

A moment later I add, "Or how about his physical ailments: first his knee, then his Achilles tendon, for a while it was his wrists and hands, then he blamed his sore butt on his seat. At times it seemed like he was popping Motrin like they were M&Ms." We laugh hard at Gary's expense and I'm sure if he were here he wouldn't have minded. All of us would have a turn at being the brunt of good-natured teasing because laughter always trumped ego.

Moments later, when the laughing stopped, it was quiet again except for the wind rushing by my ears and the clicking of the chain riding across the sprockets on my bike. Gary brings a vitality and energy to the group and it's different when he isn't with us. I was thinking back to that day in upstate New York. Mark wasn't too far off target. With Gary we are, at times, the three stooges without all the slapping and hitting, and with just two of us, we aren't.

When we get to New Town we stop for dinner, then continue down the road for a while until we find a campground. The area for tents is a large space without defined sites that has patchy grass and a few trees, which is fine, but the restroom and shower facility is run down and filthy. I don't want to touch the faucet or the sink and you couldn't pay me to sit on either of the two toilets. The showers aren't as bad but certainly not clean. We consider riding on but it's the end of the day, we're tired, and the next campsite isn't that close.

I brought sandals to use around camp and could bike in them if my tennis shoes were soaked. I wore them whenever I took a shower. On other trips I've used lightweight flip flops, which is what Mark has. I also use the sleeping bag stuff sack to put my towel and clean clothes in and hang it from the shower curtain rod. Often, campground showers don't have a clean or dry place to put those things.

At least the water is hot and I spend as little time as necessary in there. We figure there's no use complaining, we'll be gone in the morning. Beside, it didn't get that way overnight, so the operators aren't that interested in maintenance.

Once again, we are in a large area that is nearly vacant. We camp near a mixture of small trees and large brush that offers some privacy and can shield the wind if it whips up.

I wake during the night and it's raining lightly. As I fall back to sleep I'm hoping it stops by morning. In spite of the amount of rain we've had so far, a lot of it came at night and we've only had one day where it rained continuously. We certainly have been lucky and hope it stays that way.

As we break camp it's mostly sunny but heavy clouds are inching their way up from the horizon. We bike into Parshall and find a place for breakfast. The clouds move in and we put on rain gear after we leave the restaurant. Soon we're hit with a 20 minute shower, but that seems to be all the moisture the clouds can muster. We're waiting for more, but darker, low level clouds move on leaving higher, lighter gray ones.

We are heading directly east but later will be turning north, riding toward Minot. As the sky brightens we stop for a break and raingear is packed up, along with my fleece jacket.

The wind is picking up, coming from the south. Slowly the sky clears, the sun shines and the wind becomes stronger creating a formidable crosswind that resists our forward progress.

We fight the crosswind for a couple of hours, at which point I realize the hope of it dying down or changing directions seems fruitless. We stop for a break, grab the water bottles and turn our backs to the wind. "I suppose we should be thankful it's not a headwind." I say.

Mark raises his eyebrows, tightens his lips, and with a slight roll of the eyes does a kind of sideways head nod, a gesture that says, 'Yeah, it could be worse but this is rather grueling itself, and I don't know that thankful is exactly what I'm feeling right now.' He walks over to his bike and looks at his electronic speedometer.

"How far before we turn?"

"It's about 50 miles from where we camped to the turn, so I'm guessing a little over 20 miles."

Normally, with breaks, that would be about two hours of riding or less, so now we are looking at maybe three hours of tough riding depending on how hard we want to push the pace. Once we turn, the wind will be at our backs pushing us along and the ride into Minot will be fast and easy, and that's what we're looking forward to right now.

At this force, the wind seems to have substance, a tangible quality you can touch and hold. I remember a stream crossing once when I was on a long hike. The water rose from mid calf to knee deep to mid thigh as the swift current threatened to push me over and carry me away. The water was fluid, I pushed it away as I took a step forward and it quickly reshaped itself around my leg. I am now seeing the wind in the same way with mass, reshaping and forming around us. An entity, if it had conscientiousness, as irritated at us for blocking its way.

As we ride, I'm slowly counting down the miles until we turn, which seems more agonizing than not having an immediate expectation that things are going to get better at a predetermined point. In this state of mind, time drags on and the battle to move forward is like a bad dream where you are struggling with all your might but can't seem to get away from impending doom.

It's a great relief to finally spot the intersection and as I make a sweeping turn I can feel the force of the wind pick me up and push me along. Suddenly I'm riding in a vacuum, the air I'm riding through is moving along with me. There is no resistance, nothing pushing against me, no ruffled noise at my ear inhibiting sound.

I move my hands from the drop handlebar to the straight one and move my body from tense and hunkered-down to more upright and at ease. My mental state relaxes and I'm thinking ahead to dinner and camp. If the wind stays strong we should be able to cover quite a few more miles without much effort.

By the time we make it to Minot the bike shop that's listed on our touring map is closed. We had experienced a rash of flats and wanted to get some more tubes. We also want to do laundry and Mark approaches a man in a car at a stop sign, and asks for directions. It isn't far or difficult to get to, but the man repeats the directions once, then twice, then a third time with slight variations. Each time Mark says thanks and takes a step back but he doesn't turn quickly enough before the man starts talking again. The sixth time it happens is just comical and I have to resist laughing out loud. The seventh time I turn away and bit my lip. Finally the man drives on and we turn toward each other and both start laughing.

"Did you get that?" I say to Mark. "Because all you need to do is go down to the first light…" I can't finish before we're both laughing again.

After laundry we find a place to eat and then a campground that is run by a large hotel chain in a modern, high-rise building. At the front desk we ask about campsites, which are not visible from the front, and around back near a wooded area we find the tent section. Again, we're the only ones set up there.

We have breakfast in the hotel restaurant and enjoy a leisurely morning, neither of us anxious to jump on the bikes. I find a newspaper, pull off the front section and hand the rest to Mark. Over numerous coffee refills, we read through the paper a section at a time.

From Minot we'll be mostly stair-stepping our way to Fargo, heading east then south, then east, then south and on until we get there. First, there is a long ride east to Rugby where we'll turn south.

With a slight tailwind that helps push us along, warm and sunny weather, and a smooth and relatively flat road, we quickly fall into a rhythm that carries us for miles without a break. A few hours later when we stop and chow on an assortment of granola bars, candy, and dried fruit, I look down at my arms. From the top of my hands up to my shirt sleeves, my arms are a dark weathered brown. I twist my hands palm up, and underneath they are a pale, pasty white. My nose and cheeks are sun damaged with skin peeling off and I wouldn't be surprised if the back of my neck looks like a dried out, leather boot.

"I really need to get some sun screen."

"Don't you think it's a little late now?"

"Well, I'll make sure I have some for the next segment."

"Didn't you say that the last time?" We laugh.

"Hey, aren't you carrying some community-gear sunscreen?"

"I think Gary has it."

We roll into Rugby just before 5:00 p.m. and learn we are in the Geographic Center of North America. There is a monument dedicated to such a declaration and of course we stop and pose for a picture. Part of me wants to throw my hands over my head and exclaim, "Woo hoo! We've conquered the Geographical Center of North America! Oh yeah, baby!" but another part of me looks around and thinks, "Eh, not much different from any other place on the planet."

Rugby is the largest town we've come through since Minot with a population of 2909. There are a couple of places for dinner and we decide on a small café.

The riding has been pleasant today and the weather good, so after a long dinner break we decide to keep riding. The route now turns south and it'll be 30 or so miles before we get to a campsite. As we settle into a familiar cadence I lean forward and rest my elbows on my aero bar. The evening air is a little cooler and we're thankful for that but after a couple of hours I feel like I've run out of energy. Trying to find campgrounds with showers, at the moment we want to camp, has been a challenge that has grown tiresome. Further, I know the trip will end soon but I could use a rest day, a day when we just don't ride, or at least a break in our routine.

About nine miles from Esmond we turn east again and about an hour later pull into the city park to camp. It feels like it's been a long day and I check my odometer to find we've biked 101 miles. No wonder I'm drained.

The campground is near a playground and some young kids come over to watch us set up camp. I would guess the oldest is around seven and they don't get too close but are obviously fascinated by a couple of guys with strange bikes. Eventually one of the small boys walks over to Mark and in a low voice so I can't hear, asks, in reference to the wastebaskets I'm using as front panniers, "Is that guy carrying garbage?"

Later when Mark tells me we have a good laugh. The wastebaskets I'm using as front panniers are bolted to the frame I made so I don't take them off. Once the bike is stripped of the other gear, I suppose it looks quite odd to see these things attached to the front wheel.

After a shower, I crawl into the tent, zip the door behind me and plop onto my sleeping bag.

We wake to another sunny day and find a café in town for breakfast. The waitress hands us menus and brings coffee, then takes our order. There is a newspaper that's been left on another table and Mark gets up and takes it, handing me a few sections. I take a sip of my coffee and knowing Mark is getting tired of listening to me complain about this, loudly exclaim, "Ahhhh! The thrill of the swill!" We both laugh.

"So you like your coffee?" Mark says prodding me.

"Oh, it's tasty!" I respond with sarcastic enthusiasm. There are times when I think I should order something else but I always pick what I consider weak coffee over no coffee. Beside, I keep thinking there's a chance I'll finally get a stout brew, but ultimately realize it's unlikely.

We'll be heading east for 20 miles before turning south. Once we start riding we're glad to have a brisk tailwind to help us along. After turning south we fight the crosswind but it's for half the distance and soon enough we're heading east again.

The route loops north then south around the large and oddly shaped Devil's Lake. Because of all the rain, flooding in this area has washed out the road in a few places and we experience delays and construction. Some of the roads are built on what looks like manmade land bridges, a strip of dirt piled up across a section of the lake with a road on it. It is not surprising that rising water would damage such a road.

We decide to get away from the lake and construction and ride off route. We head north for a few miles to connect with Highway 2. From there we'll head east to Lakota, then south to Pekin to pick up the touring route again.

As we are riding north, I notice a car pull up to Mark and while still riding they engage in a conversation. Mark is behind me and I can see him in the mirror on the end of my handlebar. The car takes off and Mark yells "Eric. Hold up." He rides up and says, "There was a couple in a car that drove up and said they saw what looked like a duffel bag on the side of the road a ways back. They asked if it belonged to us. I told them it didn't but then checked and noticed I was missing one of my front panniers." I look down to verify that Mark is missing one of his bags. I can't resist asking an obviously unanswerable question, "How did you lose a pannier?"

"I don't know. They said it's about a mile back so I'm going to go get it. You might as well stay here, I'll be back in a second."

Mark zips back to retrieve his bag and a minor disaster is averted. I wait on the side of the road and in no time he is riding up with the missing pannier firmly attached to his bike. "Do you need some duct tape to wrap around that pannier to make sure it's nice and secure? Because I think I've got some." I jokingly say as Mark pulls up.

"Maybe you could use it to secure the lid on your plastic box so it doesn't fly away," Mark shoots back. We both laugh.

Once we're on Highway 2 we come to a campground in late afternoon that's about 60 miles from our starting point. We decide to bypass it and take our chances down the road. Even along this highway, one of the main roads in the area, there aren't many towns, and services are limited. We find a place to have dinner then a couple of hours later, a place to camp that doesn't look like a campground as much as it looks like a vacant field someone is trying to make a few extra dollars with. We stop and inquire but they don't have showers and we decide to ride on. A while later we roll into Lakota. We'll reconnect with the route in Pekin where there is a campground but it's 18 miles away and we've already come 90 today. Mark convinces me to stay in a motel we pass and frankly, he didn't have to twist my arm.

It's a nice change, not having to set up tents and unload gear. We roll the bikes into the room and grab the clean clothes we'll need without tearing everything apart. Later, we even indulge in a little TV.

Over breakfast we make a plan for the last two days. Between Lakota and Fargo, Cooperstown seems to be our best chance at finding a campsite with showers because it's the biggest town we'll ride through with a population of 1247, according to our touring map. This means that today will be a relatively short one and tomorrow a long one, somewhere around 60 and 90 miles respectively.

We'll finish the trip earlier than planned and be able to start the ride home. Our average daily mileage for the east segment was 65, and for the west it was 61, which is for the full days of riding and doesn't include a few partial days either at the beginning or end of each segment. For this trip we set our daily mileage a little higher and planned accordingly. But our average, at 79 miles a day, is higher than we thought. Once, when we had discussed this I jokingly said, "See, Gary *was* holding us back all this time!" Mark and I laughed hard knowing Gary would have serious objection to this. He was often pushing the pace, but we also seemed to stop more often when the three of us rode together.

We're heading directly south for most of the day. It's overcast and cooler and the wind has died down considerably. We are still riding through remote areas with small towns whose population is often below 1000 and sometimes below 100. It's hard to see that some of the places are actually towns because they barely consist of more than a couple of buildings.

Over the last few days as we get closer Fargo, there is a change in geography. Where trees normally stand alone or in small clusters, I'm noticing bigger stands and more of them. Acres of tall grass are turning into a rich mixture of shrubs, small trees, ferns, and big-leafed plants. The grasses of the plains are slowly giving way to the encroaching forest. As we approach the North Dakota/Minnesota border there is a physical transition between the vast open spaces of the prairie and the lush forests and lakes of the Great Lakes States. The transition is as dramatic as the one between the geology, forests and alpine meadows of the mountains and the relatively flat terrain and waist-high grasses of the plains.

It's been over an hour since our last stop. I look down at the map and there isn't any notable feature or town coming up so we pull off to the side for a break. Water bottles are pulled from their cages and the snack compartment of my pannier is unzipped.

"The number of ice cream shops, coffee houses, and diners serving homemade pie seems to be lacking on this trip," I point out to Mark. "Either that or we're not living up to our reputation." Mark smiles and nods in agreement. "Do you think you've lost any weight on this trip?" I ask.

Without hesitation, Mark says, "Nope." We laugh, and Mark asks, "How about you?"

"No," I say with a smile. "By the way, I bought another bag of those small candy bars." I pull the bag out and place it on top of the plastic box on the rear of my bike. "Help yourself."

After 58 miles we arrive in Cooperstown, which on this segment, is a short day. The road has been relatively flat and smooth and the wind was relegated to a slight breeze. Our total riding time was less than five hours.

We see a steak house and decide to stop for a laid back dinner. Later we set up camp at the city park.

I sit on the picnic table at our site, on the tabletop with my feet on the bench. I'm thinking back over the past week. We had a stretch of good days when the sun shined and the day started warm, became hot, then tapered off into a nice soothing evening, while we relaxed at our campsite, waiting for the night. I put on my fleece jacket, the air is still, and shadows grow long tinged with a golden glow.

Barring some unusual circumstance, we will ride into Fargo today and start the trip home. We'll have to cover 90 miles or more so we try to get an early start. We break camp with an air of excited anticipation.

After breakfast we're riding on a quiet, tree-lined residential street with well-kept houses and manicured yards. We're moving slowly, I'm about 10 feet in front of Mark. A short ways ahead, I watch a squirrel run down the side of a large tree, take a few hops into the street and then stop. He sees us approaching, stands up on his hind legs and then jumps back toward the curb. I stop pedaling and am moving forward at maybe two miles an hour. As I get closer it looks like he's changed his mind and is going to run across the street anyway and at the speed we're approaching, he has plenty of time. But once again he gets part way out and stops, frozen on the spot and directly in front of me. Now I'm eight feet away and closing, and the squirrel engages in an erratic dance where he moves a foot or two to my left and stops, then reverses and then back again. I haven't changed direction or speed, three feet, two feet... I'm watching him bolt back and forth taking a moment each time to watch my approaching bike as if he's mesmerized. I tense up, and in the last couple of seconds try to counter act his movements by jerking the handlebars back and forth while my body squirms, then brace for the impact not because I'm afraid for myself, but for him. At the last fraction of a second, his claws frantically scraping the asphalt, he spins around and runs back toward the curb and I roll over the lower part of his back, which only momentarily stops him as he scampers to the side of the road and up a tree.

Astonished, I turned to Mark and say, "Did you see that!"

"What?"

"I just ran over a squirrel!"

Mark looks around expecting to see road kill on the street.

"No, he's fine. After my front tire rolled over his back, he shot off to the side of the road and up a tree."

"Really? You ran over a squirrel?"

"Yeah, it was the craziest thing," still finding it hard to believe what happened. I'm stunned, unable to pedal as Mark rolls ahead. My mind is rerunning the bizarre event, bewildered at how the squirrel, with plenty of time to cross the street safely, could make a series of bad choices that ended not fatally, but with perhaps the second worst outcome. I'm still emotionally transfixed by the panic and confusion the small animal felt. It just didn't make sense, and I realize it never will.

When I come out of my fog, Mark is a ways ahead. I stand on the pedals and pick up my pace to catch up with him.

We ride out to State Road 200 and head east. Luckily there is a brisk tail wind that pushes us along. We make good time over the next 15 miles but then turn southeast and the wind is less helpful. It's much warmer by mid morning and feels like it's going to be quite hot today.

By early afternoon we head east again but then turn south and fight the cross wind, but only for seven miles. The small towns are still spaced far apart with large farms and prairie between them. The sun is shining full blast and it's hot, maybe in the 90's. We turn east and are pushed along until the final section where we turn southeast. The wind seems less strong here and I wonder if it's because of all the buildings and trees that make the outlying areas of Fargo seem overgrown.

As we make our way through the city, the route actually crosses the Red River into Minnesota for about a quarter of a mile. We are heading south on Broadway and once we cross the railroad tracks the station is just to the left.

We ride up to the truck and Mark looks for his keys while I pull out the camera and tripod. I set it up and take a picture of us by the truck, and another in front of the station. We load our gear and I check the odometer to see that we covered 94 miles, and it feels like it.

There's a restaurant near the train station and we make a beeline toward it. The air conditioning helps remove the haze from my brain as I settle into the cushy bench seat of a booth. It's a little after 5:00 p.m. and Mark and I are in good spirits having finished another segment. After dinner, we're anxious to get on the road and if we start now we can get a hotel, or camp later and finish up tomorrow.

Out on the highway the sun dims and passing cars are starting to turn on their headlights. Mark is mesmerized by the road and I gaze out the window spellbound by the passing scenery.

Memories of the trip float through my mind like leaves on a river. I bounce from the all day rain, to the thrill of being pushed by the wind and the sunset over Lake Sakakawea. In my mind I see the grassy plain spread out before me for miles on a sunny day, the tent contort and shudder in the fierce storms while I lay looking up at it, and the lonely solitude of towns so small they are represented by only a couple of buildings.

Interlude

During the summer we talk about doing the short ride through Canada that was supposed to be part of the east segment. After checking where we can cross back into the United States, we choose a route that will take us to Mark's house in the northern suburbs of Detroit. We plan to hug the northern coast of Lake Erie, then head northwest to our crossing point that will bring us back to the United States. It's not the most direct route but we're hoping it will be the most scenic and keep us off highly traveled roads. We figure the route will be around 250 miles and pick four days in mid September.

The days will be shorter and cooler, but it's still summer so it should be warm enough to enjoy the ride. There is the possibility we could run into a lot of rain at this time of the year, but this just seems to fit everyone's schedule.

The only modifications to my gear are some additions to the clothing I'll take in case the weather is cool. I have a variety of options from sweaters to vests, fleece to insulated jackets, so it's just coming up with things that can work together in layers, in case it gets really cold. I'll also take something more than shorts and rain pants for my legs, and a hat and gloves.

We won't be taking the stove, pots, cups, or any related items including food, other than snacks. Up to this point we have only used the stove a few times, and that was because we were in a remote area without a restaurant nearby. It seems improbable on this segment that we won't be able to find plenty of places to eat. Ditching this gear will save weight and give us some extra room for added clothing.

We'll be off route, that is, off the route of the touring maps we're using. Aside from some problems with traffic and congestion around

Rochester, the couple of days we were off route on the east segment were inconvenient, sometimes a hassle, but not a problem to the point where we considered buying more detailed maps this time. We'll use standard road maps that only show main highways and secondary streets, but figure they'll be good enough to find a decent route.

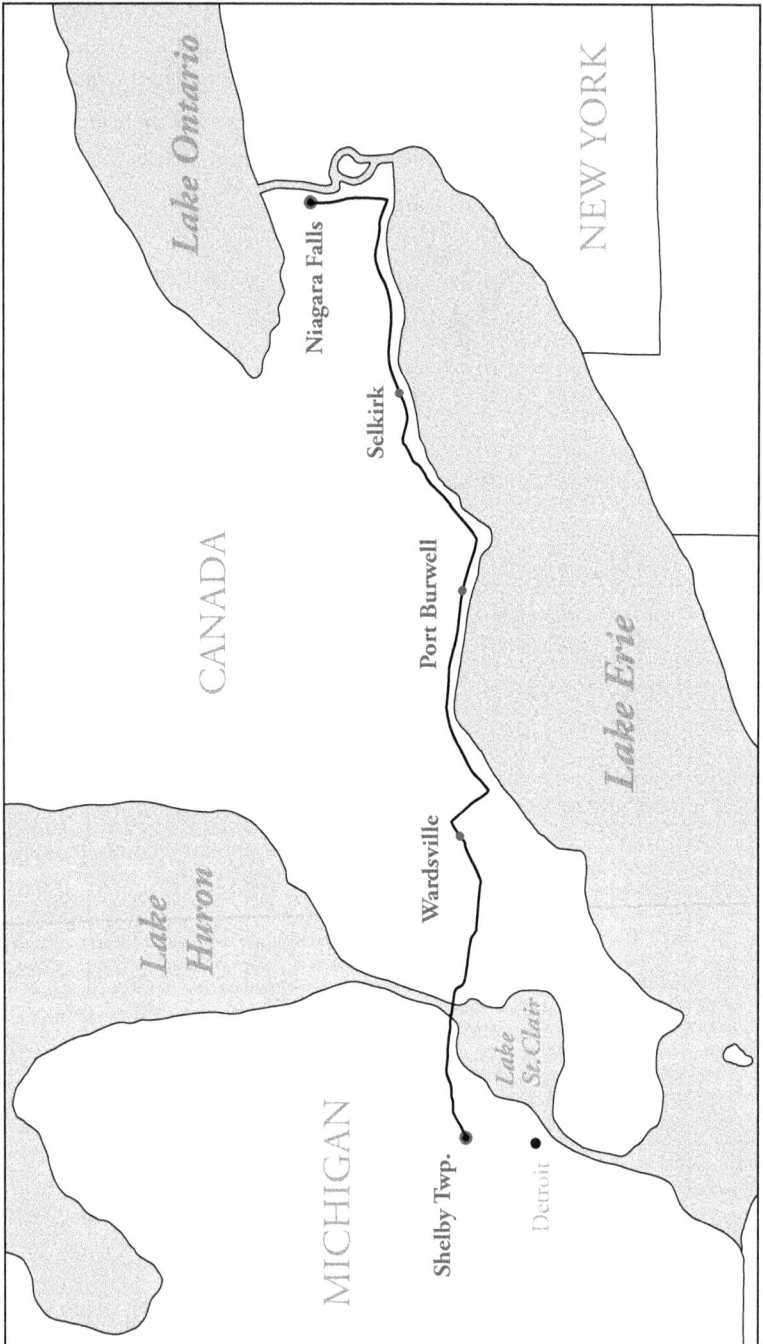

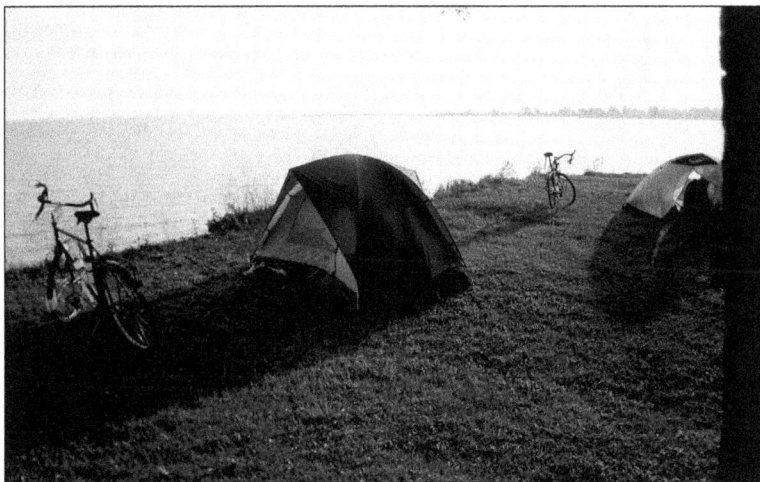

Canada

"I thought this route would be a little more scenic," I say as Mark and I ride side by side.

"Me too. I'm surprised we haven't been able to see Lake Erie more often."

The three of us are making our way along roads that are as close to Lake Erie as we can find on our crude maps, but the view is often obstructed by trees so the road doesn't have to be very far inland to prevent us from seeing the lake. So far, we've had only brief views, without public access, and are riding mostly through forested land broken up by small towns and farms.

Just after midnight we arrive in the city of Niagara Falls and find the campground where we have reservations. Gary's dad, Bob, generously volunteered to take us back to the point where we left off, where he had picked us up two years ago. We decided to drive out on a Friday evening, after work, then ride back over the next four days.

Tents are set up as we try not to disturb the other campers who all seem to be sleeping. I was expecting it to be cold and had brought some extra clothes, but it's cool at best and I didn't notice the temperature until I started digging through my panniers and found the extra gear. Now it seems like some of this stuff is excessive. I have a hat and gloves, and a scarf too. I have lightweight long underwear for my legs, and also a pair of fleece pants. I have a fleece jacket and lightweight sweater, and also a down vest. As I sift through my bags by flashlight, it looks as if I've brought a lot more food than I really need too. Just when I thought I had developed a routine that pared my weight to the essentials, a little too much reckless abandon resulted in a load that's heavier than it needs to be. There always seems to be a fine balance between carrying something that you never use versus being caught without something you need, and without taking a moment to scrutinize an item it's just easier to throw it in your bag. Pretty soon ounces turn to pounds and you're kicking yourself for not being more judicious.

Once I have things organized I shake my down sleeping bag to fluff it up and lay my head on the fleece jacket I'm using as a pillow. Minutes later I'm out.

Considering the late night, we're still up at a fairly early hour. After we stop to eat, Bob drives us to the parking lot near the Skylon Tower, which is where we ended the east segment. After he wishes us a safe trip, and vice versa, Bob heads back toward Detroit and we head directly south so we can pick up Highway 3, which runs west along the lake. From the rough maps we have it's hard to tell how close to the shore we can get because it's possible there are secondary roads that aren't shown that will provide the best route.

We have sketchy information about campgrounds too, but figure we can ask locals for suggestions and this trip is short enough so that any inconvenience won't be a big problem.

Highway 3 is a busier, provincial road but after 20 miles it splits and we take local road 3, which mimics the curves of the shoreline. Unfortunately we're too far inland to see the lake. This road is much less traveled and we ride side by side for a long time. Small towns and numerous farms are interspersed with thick, overgrown forest. Fields have been harvested or hold crops that have become brown or yellowed. It's still summer, technically, so the trees are mostly green even though we've had some cold nights.

The road is eventually pushed north by the Grand River until we come to a bridge and cross it. The day is cool, yet warm enough to ride in shorts and a light jacket. It's sunny, but a hazy sunny. It's as if, after a long summer at full blast, the sun is just a little tired and doesn't have the strength to shine as bright. The traffic is very light and when necessary, we ride on the edge of the road because the shoulder is gravel. As cars pass they give us a wide berth.

After lunch we have the opportunity to take a road that looks as if it will put us closer to the view were searching for. The map shows that the road we're on is considerably inland, so we decide to take the alternate. We're thinking that even if this isn't the best route, as long as we keep moving west we'll be making progress toward our goal. After an hour we haven't seen the lake and not surprisingly we get to a point where we're pretty sure we're lost. Mark waves down a vehicle to get help. Knowing I'm not good with audible directions I let Mark and Gary talk to the driver. The elderly couple is quite nice, give us a lot of information and eventually we make it back to 3 no better or worse for our off-the-beaten-path sojourn.

So far, finding great views of Lake Erie has been a challenge, and while we haven't given up on the idea, we're certainly less optimistic about it.

In Selkirk we have dinner, then make our way to Selkirk Provincial Park. We arrive in the evening after a decent ride, 73 miles. The days are shorter now, the sun is setting around 7:30 p.m. and in order to avoid riding after dark we have to make an effort to keep track of our time and progress throughout the day. We are all aware of this and I don't think anyone wants to revive the tired, old argument about riding after dark.

The campground is nice, heavily wooded, and there is hardly anyone here. There's not a shred of grass at our campsite and we set up on dirt covered with a spotty blanket of oak leaves and pine needles. There is enough daylight left to take a shower and settle in before dark.

After the sun dips below the horizon, the air develops a colder bite. Inside my tent I wrap the sleeping bag around me and use the flashlight to chart our progress. Then I scribble some notes about the trip and snack on peanut M&Ms before balling my fleece jacket into a pillow and retiring for the night.

At breakfast we look ahead on the map and find only one campground that is approximately a day's ride away. It will be a little short in terms of mileage but there doesn't appear to be any other campgrounds for quite a ways after that. However, it's possible that once we get there we might come across someone that can point us to a spot a bit further down the road.

Making our way with basic road maps certainly isn't the most optimal way to proceed, but carrying detailed topographical or county maps, if we could get them, seems like overkill. There isn't an easy solution and on a short trip like this, not finding the best route or prime campsites is more of an inconvenience than a problem. So far the route is pleasant, traffic mild, the countryside nice, but with the expectation of a shoreline ride, it seems a little disappointing.

We head west and in order to follow the coast there are a number of turns and we spend a short amount of time on a variety of roads. While trying to stay off the main roads, the secondary ones sometimes twist around and aren't always easy to follow. We have another chance to ride closer to the shore, and again take a local road not on our map as it curves toward the coast. We're able to catch a glimpse of the lake on occasion, but there's no public access and the road eventually ends. The lake is in sight and there is a trail that heads into the forest so we hike down it a ways to see if it's passable. It's not, and we backtrack to find a road that will take us west.

After lunch we pass through Turkey Point Provincial Park and pass Long Point peninsula. As the afternoon wears on we find a place for dinner near Port Burwell. A little further down the road, just east of Port Burwell Provincial Park, we find a campground and can see Lake Erie about 50 yards away through the trees. We decide to camp there. The tent area doesn't have designated sites and we walk the bikes toward the lake. We find a spot with a few large trees that don't obscure the panoramic view and we pitch our tents near the edge of an abrupt drop off into the lake. The day was cool, but sitting in the sun with no perceptible wind makes the evening feel much warmer.

I go take a shower, then get out my camera as the sun sets. The lake is relatively calm but the surface shimmers as shadows grow long and twilight darkens the sky.

We wake to a cool morning and overcast skies. After breakfast the road jogs north before heading west, so again we are too far inland to see the coast. We ride through Lakeview and Copenhagen before the road turns back toward the lake and Port Bruce. But after Port Bruce the highway curves inland again before heading west.

It's been cooler than the previous days and looks like rain but so far we've been lucky. We ride into Port Stanley, see a small diner and stop for coffee. We're not exactly hungry for a meal but after a look at the desert menu, we indulge in cheesecake. I don't know if it's possible for us to stop at a diner and not have something to eat. Mentioning this to Mark and Gary brings a round of laughter.

We've been disagreeing over our route since morning. From Port Stanley, we are almost directly east of where we are going to cross back into the United States. Gary wants to make a beeline toward there. The coast curves southwest and Mark and I want to stay close and camp near Morpeth, which seems a bit out of the way. Yet, even if we try to head directly west at this point, there are no east/west roads. As the coast curves, roads run either parallel or perpendicular to the coast, so trying to head directly east would mean stair-stepping: heading southwest, then northwest, then southwest, then northwest until we get to the roads that run directly west. In miles, it doesn't seem like one route is that much closer than the other.

After a number of refills we leave the diner and come across a rack with brochures of local attractions. Mark looks through the selection for a detailed map of the area and finds one. We huddle up and take a look at it. The road on our provincial map heads northwest then southwest but we see that there is a more direct route and take off in that direction. We continue down the coast as it curves southwest until we stop at a café in Eagle. Again, we resist anything substantial but indulge in the good stuff, homemade pie.

With the new map comes another option that is not on our provincial maps. There is a conservation area that allows camping and isn't too far out of the way. There are no showers but it's closer than Morpeth. Since it's already late afternoon, getting to our original destination before dark doesn't seem feasible. We decide to head to the conservation area.

A few hours later we stop for dinner then go find the campground. We arrive at Big Bend Conservation Area at dusk and have the place to ourselves. By the time the tents go up it's dark and as I pull out my sleeping bag and dig through one of the pockets of my panniers for some dried fruit, I hear the throaty roar of what sounds like a couple of big pick-up trucks racing around the area. Soon I can see flicker of headlights through the trees on the side of the tent wall and hear the whoops and hollers of joyriders. In the position I'm sitting, the road into the conservation area is on the right. It comes to the edge of the camping area then loops around and goes back out. Directly in front of me and adjacent to the camping area is a large field. Heavy forest is to the left and behind. As the sound of the trucks come closer, the headlights pan across the tents as they drive by. Then it sounds like they're off the road at the distant edge of the field in front of me. A moment later the headlights are on us as the sound of the roar increases and one of the trucks barrels in our direction. I'm tensed up, poised to run when the headlights dip and I hear the tires slide on the grass. I imagine what a deer, crossing the road at night and confronted by a car, must feel like.

"Hey! Who's there!" a shout comes from the truck.

Seriously? We're going to be harassed by some high school kids? I think as I become defiant.

"Who's asking?" I shout back.

"I'm Bill and I've got Gina with me."

Okay, let's go with it. "I'm Eric, and I'm riding with Mark and Gary. We're from Detroit and we're biking from Niagara Falls back home."

There is a short pause then, "That's cool. Have a good trip."

The engine roars, the headlights pan away and in a few moments it's quiet again.

"I thought we were going to have trouble for a second," Gary says while still inside his tent.

"Yeah, I really wasn't sure what was going to happen, but I wasn't expecting that."

We're up early because we know it will be a long day. After breakfast we head in a southwestern direction through Thamesville and then head directly west. Gary is out front pushing the pace and we're covering a lot of miles in a short time.

It's overcast and cool. I had put on my hat and gloves, but riding at a brisk pace warmed me up. I think about taking them off, but the air is still cool and my cheeks and nose are cold. At a short break I take off my gloves and warm my face with my hands. Mark sees me and says, "The air is a bit nippy, isn't it?" Mark's cheeks are rosy as well.

"Whenever I ride in conditions like this I always think I should get one of those face masks, but I never do. I have a scarf with me but the condensation that forms around your nose and mouth is a hassle. Then you're just sucking on a wet rag."

"Yeah. Maybe it will warm up a little later."

We're determined to get home and resist the urge to stop for too long or duck into a café or diner. Staying focused pays off, we cover nearly 40 miles before noon, a record for us.

When we get closer to the border, we check the map and veer north into Wallaceburg then turn west and eventually cross the bridge onto Walpole Island and head toward the ferry terminal.

It's a short ride back into the United States at Algonac, crossing the Saint Clair River at the southern end as it splits up and spills into Lake Saint Clair. We find a place to stop for lunch and when finished, I search my wallet for some American money and stash the Canadian bills to exchange later.

We ride on Highway 29 as it curves around Anchor Bay and changes names from Dyke Road to Point Tremble Road to Dixie Highway to Main Street in New Baltimore, then splits and merges with 23 Mile Road.

Just past New Baltimore, Gary takes off for his parent's house and Mark and I ride toward Mark's house. It's just south of 23 Mile Road and about 20 miles west, but riding on this busy street isn't pleasant so we try to find parallel roads that snake through subdivisions. This leads us through areas of minimal traffic but we often find the roads curve around and spit us back out on 23 Mile. At other times we arrive at a dead end and once, the paved road we're on ends and we continue on rough, muddy gravel that takes us through a wooded, undeveloped area. We pass subdivisions where all roads loop around and come back to where you started. We are constantly looking for a better route and at times, when the shoulder disappears, are forced up on the sidewalk, when there is a sidewalk, or over grass. The last part of this segment proved to be difficult and tiresome riding. By the time we make it to Mark's it's 6:00 p.m. and we never thought it would take that long. Exhuasted, I throw my bike and gear in the car, spend a few minutes talking to Mark, then head toward home.

Interlude

During the winter we set the dates for the last segment, the one that will take us from Fargo, North Dakota, to Metro Detroit, through Minnesota, Wisconsin, and Michigan's Upper and Lower Peninsula to complete our trip. We decide to ride in the spring again, starting in mid June, to take advantage of the long days. To get to Fargo, we'll take the train from Detroit, connecting from the commuter train in Chicago to the Empire Builder. Gary made arrangements to bike with us through the first 10 days, then meet up with his wife and daughter to spend time at a friend's cabin.

Since Mark and I are ending the trip at his house, our schedule will be a bit more flexible. We won't have to be at a specific destination at a certain time and there are enough days set aside so we won't have to rush to the end or be too concerned about mileage.

Much of the route on this segment is not covered by the touring maps we've been using. This was a bit of an issue in Canada and on the east segment. Searching for a campground or riding on busy streets was a nuisance, but looking back it didn't seem like a big deal. Besides, the only alternative we can think of is something none of us are thrilled about, carrying a large collection of topographical or county maps. We figure the state maps will be good enough, without spending much time talking about it.

Again, we decide to leave behind the stove, fuel, pots, cups, silverware and meal-type food for snack food and restaurants. In retrospect, we probably could have done this earlier without a problem. Although we carried the stove on a good part of the trip we just didn't use it that often. For example, we could have had a warm drink in the morning or evening, but it wasn't part of our routine and we didn't consider it.

I don't know if we ever used the stove for anything other than heating water, and we could have done that with a fire, although we didn't build one very often either. When we did use it, we could have eaten snack food instead, which wouldn't have been an issue since it didn't happen that often.

There are no changes to the system I figured out for carrying gear. I like using the plastic boxes, one on top of my rear rack for the foam pad, fleece jacket, wind jacket and miscellaneous things. Two for the front panniers, one holding the tent and the other for the sleeping bag and one for the handlebars that holds my camera and money and has a map holder on top. Also, each of my rear panniers now has a large pocket to hold small gear.

There are some minor changes to the kind of clothing each of us will bring, and small adjustments to some other gear, but nothing noteworthy.

For each segment I made a copy of my gear list that included items I considered but didn't take and simply crossed off so I knew exactly what I took each time. When I finished a segment I wrote some notes about what worked and what didn't and kept the paperwork together in a big envelope so I could refer to it before the next trip. This way, what I took evolved over a period of time until I had a system I was comfortable with.

Eventually, I realized many things can be bought on the road if you happen to forget, lose, or decide not to carry something then change your mind. Also, I found it's easy to become preoccupied with picking the most appropriate gear and finding the balance between weight and necessity, but it's important not to become obsessed or let yourself believe that your selection of gear is the most important aspect of a trip.

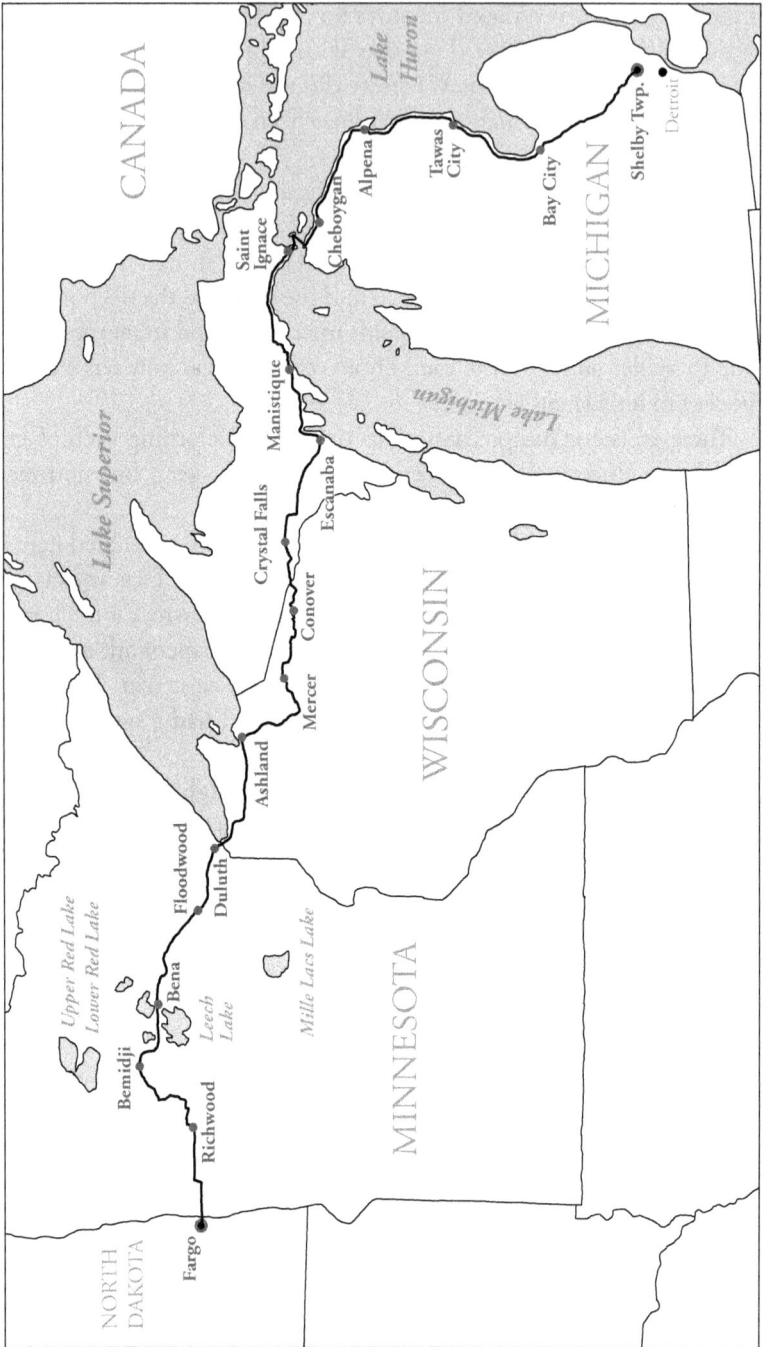

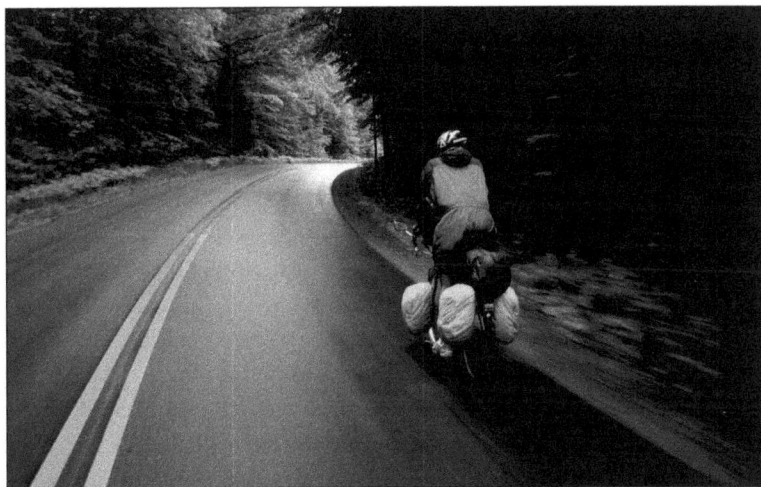

Great Lakes

"Oh my God, it's cold!" I blurt out almost involuntarily, grimacing as I step off the train and scramble to zip up my fleece jacket. It's early morning and we've just arrived in Fargo, North Dakota, and although it's June this is clearly the coldest it's been on the entire trip. The weather looked deceptively nice as we pulled up to the station so it's quite a surprise to be hit with a cold blast of arctic air as I step outside. I quickly pull out my rain gear and put it on as we're waiting for our bikes and other gear to be unloaded.

I meet Mark and Gary at the Dearborn, Michigan train station a little after 6:30 a.m., early enough to check our gear with a cushion for potential mishaps. The train is scheduled to leave at 7:11 and we're told it's running on time. The three of us are riding from Dearborn, in the suburbs of Detroit, to Fargo, North Dakota, where Mark and I ended the plains segment of the trip.

After we check our gear, we sit in the waiting area. Gary brought a small video camera and while filming, asks me how much gear I'm carrying, then once again makes a comment about how he has to haul all the community gear. Mark chimes in and says, "We haven't even got on the train yet and the whining has started," and we all laugh. I haven't seen Gary in a few months and give him a hard time about his plan to ride only half way through this segment, and we continue to poke fun at each other while we wait.

The train is on time and we board for the nearly five hour ride to Chicago. This is the commuter train that runs between Detroit and Chicago, where we'll transfer to the Empire Builder for the ride to Fargo. We find seats, then head to the lounge car where we can face each other and talk. Around 11:30 we pull into Union Station in Chicago. There is a 2½ hour lay over.

We leisurely wander through the old, grandiose station then head to the modern, lower level, where the trains board. There are plenty of concessions and we find something to eat. When it gets close to our departure time we walk over to the staging area. Just when we think we're about to board, there are further delays and we stand in the crowded waiting room for another hour. Once we make it through the gate, we walk down the platform, and climb up the steps of the Empire Builder.

The train is pretty full and Gary and Mark slide into a couple of seats next to each other and I sit behind them. We settle in for a 14 hour ride. I've brought a couple of magazines that I'll leave behind and page through one as the train departs. Gary suggests we head to the observation car where it will be easier to talk. We're all in good spirits, happy to be on vacation and excited about this segment. It's late afternoon as the train makes its way out of the city and rolls through the suburbs as it heads north.

When the conductor announces the dining car will open soon, we get up and make our way forward to stand in line with a handful of other diners. We're seated in a booth that can accommodate four, and order. I keep thinking of those old black and white movies, like North by Northwest, and the scenes where the characters are in the dining car. All the men are in a suit and tie, women in fine dresses of the latest fashion. The place settings are formal with linen napkins. Today's dining car is much more casual, as are its patrons, dressed in jeans and t-shirts, sweat pants and sweat shirts, halter tops and shorts.

We make our way through Wisconsin and cross the Minnesota border late in the evening. As people get on and off the train at various stops, each of us moves so that we can have two empty seats to ourselves. The seats have been reupholstered since the last time Mark and

I were on it and are more comfortable. Still, I'm glad to have my foam pad, the one I sleep on, to make the seat extra cushy. I am wearing shorts and t-shirt and had put my fleece jacket on over it. As I prepare to nod off, I put on my rain pants and jacket for extra warmth.

Much later, I wake briefly and find I am turned toward the window. It's dark, but there is enough light in the car to create a reflection and prevent me from seeing outside. I lean forward and place my forehead against the glass blocking the light with my right hand at my temple. The barren landscape comes into view. It's raining hard, I can see the blurry haze because of some distant lights. This is not what I was hoping for. I lean back and shut my eyes. A minute later I'm out.

I wake to darkness and dimmed lights in a quiet railcar. I reach into my pocket and pull out my electronic speedometer to look at the time. It's 5:30 a.m. and something's not right. In my post sleep haze I look around for the other guys in a slight sense of panic but everyone is slumped down and sleeping. It should be dark, that makes sense, but our arrival time is 3:39 a.m., or now, 4:39 a.m. with the hour delay in Chicago. As my ability to reason sharpens, I know that neither the conductor nor the guys would let me sleep through my stop. Most likely the train had other delays. I'm thinking it would be fortuitous if we arrive in daylight, it will be easier to put the bikes together and find a place to eat. I slump back down and nod off.

The train arrives a little after 6:00 a.m. It's daylight, overcast, but no rain. Everything looks good until we get off the train. The temperature feels like it's in the 30s with a wind chill factor far below that. Luckily, the station manager let us assemble the bikes inside. Before we roll out the door I bundle up and put socks on my hands as mittens. We quickly find a place for breakfast.

The route on the touring map starts in Fargo, heads to Grand Rapids, Minnesota and turns south. We'll continue east into Wisconsin. About halfway through the state we'll pick up another of the touring routes and take that into the Upper Peninsula of Michigan until we reach the Mackinac Bridge, which connects the Upper and Lower Peninsulas. Then we'll be off route again, all the way back to the Detroit area, riding along the east coast of the state.

After breakfast we brave the cold again. None of us packed cold-weather clothing so we pile on what we have. Over my t-shirt, I put on a lightweight fleece vest, then my fleece jacket and light wind shell, then rain gear over that, including rain pants. Instead of a hat, which is bulky under the helmet, I brought a fleece headband, that goes on under my hood and I put socks on my hands. With the heat my body generated from biking I was fine but stopping for any length of time made me wish I had brought a down jacket.

Just like East Glacier, Montana, is the point where mountains turn to plains, Fargo, North Dakota, seems to be the place were the plains turn into the many lakes and lush green forests of the Great Lakes Region. Almost from the start, the landscape seems overgrown with trees and brush, and gone are the wide-open vistas.

It's gray, dim and cold all morning. We move along at a good pace over relatively flat terrain and lightly traveled back roads but our spirits are dampened slightly by the dreary weather. We stop for a few breaks and indulge in granola bars, dried fruit and candy until early afternoon when Gary says, "Hey Blue, looks like pie!" as he fixates on a small diner.

"Sure am glad we've got Gary back to find the pie shops for us," I say to Mark as we laugh. It's warm inside as we enjoy hot coffee and fresh apple pie. We sit through numerous refills, none of us anxious to get back out in the cold.

Once we resume riding, the sky grows darker and before long we're hit with a short rain shower. I quickly peel the socks off my hands not wanting them to get wet and stuff them in a pocket. I flip up my hood and feel the cool air and wet rain sting my hands. Luckily it's a short rain and the sun comes out about a half hour later. Unfortunately that is also short lived. The air temperature had warmed but we were subjected to more rain in small bursts throughout the afternoon.

We stop in Richwood for dinner and after a nice rest ride 14 miles to camp near Strawberry Lake.

Once in camp I stand in the shower and let the hot water take the chill out of my bones. I walk back to my tent at twilight and can hear Gary sleeping already. He had said he didn't get much rest on the train so it isn't surprising he's out. I'm thinking about building a campfire but the late evening air is cold and I'm tired too. I pull my sleeping bag out of its stuff sack and shake it hoping to make it as fluffy and warm as possible. I sit on the foam pad, wrap the sleeping bag around me and put my headband back on. As it gets dark, I use the flashlight to write some notes and take a look at the route for the next couple of days before retiring.

"Hey, are you little girls going to get up soon?" Gary says.

It's early and overcast so it's hard to tell what time it is. It sounds like Gary is taking down his tent. I don't want to move, it's downright frigid. My cheeks and nose are cold and I can see my breath. On the entire trip it's never been this cold.

"Hey, take a look at this. There's frost on the seats of the bikes," Gary says, "And the picnic table is covered too."

I can believe it. As Gary continues to pack up his gear I sit up and put on my rain pants and jacket, then slip on my shoes and grab my camera.

"Are you guys going to sleep all day or are we going to ride?" Gary says with a smile on his face. I unzip the door of my tent and step outside. "Some of us didn't go to bed at 7:00 last night."

Gary and I chuckle, he's in good spirits but tensed up from the cold and moving quickly. "Look at the bikes."

I walk over and take a few photos.

"I'm going to ride up to the place where we registered to get some coffee and sweet rolls they told us about last night," Gary says to me, then shouting over at Mark's tent, "Hey, Blue. Sweet rolls. Hopefully there will be some left by the time you get there." The three of us are chuckling as Gary rides away.

I jump back into my tent and bundle up with nearly every piece of clothing I have with me. When my gear is packed, I unzip the tent door and step outside with my panniers in hand. I snap them onto my bike. The grass is crunchy and I notice there are frozen drops of water on the tent canopy. "It is June, isn't it?" I say to Mark.

"Yeah."

"June, 18th, or something like that?"

"Yeah, the 17th I think."

"A few days from the beginning of summer?"

Mark chuckles, "Yeah."

"I hope it doesn't snow."

We ride up to where Gary is. The first thing I notice when I walk through the door is the warmth of the heated building. Gary is sitting at a small table. There is a big pot of coffee on the counter and some rolls next to it.

I'm chilled and don't unzip my jacket while I sip hot coffee. We start talking about the route. Gary is pushing for a 100 mile day. "After what you guys did on the plains, that's nothing," he says.

"You should have come with us," Mark says. "We did a 100 miles, like..." he pauses for a second then tries to say with a straight face, "every day!" We burst out laughing.

As we leave the campground I put clean socks on my hands again. I have my headband on, my hood up and put my helmet over both. My toes are numb and the only sound I can hear is the rustle of my rain pants as I pedal. I'm mostly looking down trying to avoid the wind chill factor of cold air slapping my face.

Under overcast skies we make our way east. We'll travel in that direction for the next few hours until we turn north and head toward Lake Itasca. This lake and the small rivers that feed it, is the source of the Mississippi River. Gary is excited to be going there and fascinated by the idea that something thrown into the lake would eventually make its way thousands of miles downriver to the Gulf of Mexico. This, of course, is the ideal scenario. It assumes that a log, for example, would not get caught on debris along the way or forced up on the riverbank or become saturated and sink. Still, he talks about this for quite a while.

As we ride, it's warming up. By late morning, I strip off the rain jacket, headband and socks that are on my hands but still have my wind jacket and fleece on. By noon the rain pants come off too. At this point we're heading north and by early afternoon we stop at Lake Itasca State Park. After a little sightseeing we head to the lodge for lunch. After a hearty meal we peruse the dessert menu and each of us indulge in a large dessert. Later, as Gary rummages through a pannier, Mark and I decide to walk over to a viewing platform that extends into the lake, about 20 yards away.

"Here, take some video," Gary says as he holds out his small video camera. When we get to the platform, I shoot a sweeping panorama of the lake and we come up with a funny idea.

Mark and I work out the details then I start the camera rolling to a close-up of Mark's hand holding a stick about the size of a 4 inch pencil. "This stick, thrown in the lake, will flow through the headwaters of the Mississippi all the way down to the Gulf of Mexico. Let's watch it!"

I continue filming as Mark throws the small stick in the lake. I follow the path of the stick until it plops in the water, then zoom in on it. Nothing happens. In the background you can hear our muffled laughter and guffaws. We're straining to hold it in, but can't. After about 15 seconds, Mark says, "Well it's not going too fast right now but sooner or later it will head down to the Gulf of Mexico." Mark can't finish the sentence without substantial effort to suppress a fit of laughter.

We end the video a minute later after much off-camera laughing, and the stick is approximately where it had been when Mark threw it in. Then we walk back.

Gary is standing by the bikes. "Did you guys shoot some video?" Mark and I are trying to hide our mischievous smiles. "Yeah, we got a little."

We continue north, then northwest as the road squiggles through the forest around lakes and streams. According to our touring map, there is only one town in the next 30 miles, Becida, population 10. Traffic is light and we alternate between riding abreast and single file.

The sun had been out briefly but now it's getting dark and eventually we are hit with a hard rain that lasts about 15 minutes. As we get closer to Bemidji it looks like more rain is imminent and eventually it falls in a measured and consistent manner as if it's going to be around for a while. But just before we reach town we are hit with a deluge and it rains hard through dinner. As we finish eating it stops and we find a campground just outside of town. Everything is wet, but luckily we are able to set up and settle in without dodging raindrops.

There is a heavy rain throughout the night. I wake a few times, turn on the flashlight and check for leaks before nodding out again. It seems like it comes down hard for hours. Toward morning, before it gets light, I find a steady drip coming from the peak of my domed tent. It had been falling on my sleeping bag but most of it rolled off and onto the floor. I move to the side and mop up a small puddle with a tiny piece of worn out towel that I had brought for such an occasion. I grab the lid of my plastic box and turn it upside down to use as a shallow basin to catch the leak, then making sure there is no more water in the tent, nod off again.

When it's time to get up, the rain had stopped but everything outside is saturated. I check for moisture along the base of the walls where the sides are sewn to the floor but everything looks all right. Before packing the tent I dry off the middle of the canopy with some tissue and place a piece of duct tape on it. I'm thinking that if we don't get much rain it will probably hold.

We ride back into Bemidji for breakfast and afterward, as we were making our way out of town, I see a hardware store and think about getting a small, cheap tarp to put over my tent. It almost seems like overkill and I quickly try to weigh the misery of being wet against carrying an extra piece of gear for the rest of the trip and never using it.

"Hey guys, hold up," I yell out. "I want to see if I can get a small tarp. Just in case."

It's warmer than it had been and I'm only wearing my wind shell over a t-shirt. The sky is cloudy, like it had been on most of the trip so far, but we're hoping we'll see sunshine today. We're heading east toward Pennington, population 60, on a lightly traveled back highway and it will be the first town we see in the next 20 miles. The road snakes through tall stands of pine and the kind of thick, overgrown brush that we had not experienced since we were in western Washington.

It isn't long before the sky grows dark and at the first sign of raindrops we scramble to grab the rain gear and put it on. The hard rain doesn't last long but saturates everything. Within a half hour the sky lightens and eventually the sun shines, but just as quickly a new storm moves in and we get rained on again.

So far the route has been hilly but not unusually so and adjusting to the terrain isn't an issue. The climbs have been gradual and relatively easy, the descents are gentle and provide ample coasting.

We reach Pennington and at a small bar, drenched and tired, but mostly just fed up with the cold, soggy weather, we certainly don't look very elite, or much like the upbeat and jovial Elite, either. It's not that we're discouraged, but the start of this segment has been challenging. Warm coffee and a dry place to sit are a temporary relief but not a permanent solution to the damp cold that had crept inside us.

Later in the afternoon we experience more bursts of rain but our spirits are lifted toward the end of the day when the clouds move on and the sun comes out. Just before we reach Bena, we see a great roadside attraction and stop to pose for a picture. It's a building that looks like a giant muskellunge. The structure has to be about 15 feet high by 60 or more feet long. The mouth is open and there are foot long teeth lining its jaws. You would enter through a door that's just inside the mouth as if you were being swallowed. There doesn't seem to be a practical use for the building, but it's always delightful finding things like this.

From there it's a short ride into town where we find a place to eat, then a campground where we can do laundry and build a campfire. As daylight fades, thick clouds of Mayflies dance in the air, their tiny transparent wings reflecting the sunlight like glitter. Our clothes are clean, the tents are dry, and staring into the fire is a calming way to end the day. In spite of a damp and dreary start, at this point everything is good and we are optimistically anticipating a stretch of warm, sunny days ahead.

We wake to overcast and cool weather but the sun intermittently comes out as we're breaking camp. By mid morning a large dose of sun warms me enough to shed my jacket and ride in just a t-shirt for the first time in four days. The warmth and bright rays feel good as the air becomes crisp and dry, and intensifies the smell of pine as we ride through thick forest.

We arrive in Grand Rapids for lunch. The touring route heads south from here toward Minneapolis, but we're heading southeast toward Duluth and the Wisconsin border, at the western tip of Lake Superior, so we'll be relying on state maps for a while.

After lunch, the sun is still with us but the wind kicks up considerably and we fight a brisk headwind. We had planned to stay at a campsite 80 miles away that morning and now, fighting the wind, we anticipate a tough ride for the rest of the day. At least we have dry, sunny weather. That is, until it clouds up, mid afternoon. And dark ominous thunderheads slowly creep in from the horizon over the tree tops. Still, I'm telling myself, 'It might not rain.' And then shortly after that, when I figure it probably will, 'Well, at least it's warm.'

Unfortunately my optimistic spin didn't prevent the inevitable.

The dark clouds move overhead and a harsh, violent storm ensues. The temperature plunges, everything is drenched. We scramble off the road and 15 minutes later it stops. 20 minutes after that everything brightens and the sun weakly appears. As fast moving clouds race across the sky it's as if the sun is on a dimmer switch that someone is playing with. Full blast intensity quickly dims down to shadowless gray, then back up, then down to dull overcast.

I've noticed that after a storm like this, there is often a dramatic change in the wind. It blows harder or calms down or changes direction. Apparently it doesn't change at all sometimes and we continue to battle a headwind for the rest of the afternoon. The air stays cool but partly sunny skies help dry the pavement and brush, and take the moisture out of the air.

We battle forward and toward the end of the day we're exhausted. We stop at a campground on the edge of Floodwood.

There's been enough rain so far that I'm happy to be setting up a dry tent. Throwing the small tarp over the canopy has now become part of my routine. Even if the duct tape holds, and no other leaks develop, having peace of mind during a heavy rain is worth the couple of seconds it takes to secure it. I throw the rest of my gear in the tent, roll out the foam pad, pull out the sleeping bag and lay down. I have to fight the urge to sleep when I really need to go take a shower. Later, I'm out in a minute.

It rained hard during the night and stays with us, lingering, as we break camp and start to ride. We follow Highway 2 toward Duluth, a busy, noisy, divided road with two lanes for each direction. The shoulders are wide and smooth but after riding through remote, quiet, back roads the congestion is bothersome.

The rain continues and at times turns into a hazy, foggy mist. The rush of traffic, one car after another, creates an oscillating rumble that drones on through the morning and into the afternoon. We don't talk much, with the hood up and the sound of the traffic, it's hard to hear. We just plod forward toward the Minnesota-Wisconsin border.

As we come into Duluth it's early evening and we look for a place to eat. The rain had let up but we still haven't seen the sun all day. Our crude maps don't offer much detail and the quickest route through the city seems to be the road we were on, Highway 2.

After dinner, we set our sights on Superior, Wisconsin, which is on the other side of a long bridge that spans Saint Louis Bay. On the map, the bridge looks like any other, a short span across a body of water. When we get to the point where we can see that Highway 2 and Interstate 35 combine and we won't be able to ride on that road, we can also see the bridge. It snakes across the bay and looks as if it could be 2 miles long. We head in that direction along city streets until we see an entry to the bridge. Once on it, the bridge eventually narrows and we realize bikes are probably prohibited. At this point however, it's too late to turn around. Luckily, motorists are accommodating as we try to sprint across, but many cars pass before we reach the other side.

We enter the small town of Superior, and make our way along city streets. Our campground information is sketchy and there is a discussion about looking for a motel versus our ability to find a place to camp. Gary wants to ask around and see if there's something in town. From the information we have, it looks like there's a place to camp up the road and I'm pushing for that. We decide to go on. Highway 53 combines with 2 and we ride that past the city boundary. Miles pass and it's getting late while apprehension builds as we realize the minimal information we have might not be entirely accurate. The further we get from the city the fewer buildings we see and there are long stretches of forest. A few miles later a roadside sign indicates camping at the next exit and we find the campground. And it has a hot tub, sauna, and small pool.

We set up the tents, unpack our gear then soak in the hot tub. As the air cools, the clouds break to reveal the last rays of sun for the day.

It's sunny as I come out of a deep sleep, the first time that's happened on this trip, the first time in six days, but there are clouds to the west. I hear the other guys rousing and start to pack up. Breaking down his tent, Gary looks upward and scanning the sky says, "I hope this is a good omen."

We stay on State Road 13, a far less traveled road than 2, heading directly east before turning south. It's a 15 mile ride into Poplar where we stop for breakfast. Along the way, the clouds have moved in and cut off the sun. By the time we're finished eating, it's raining. I take a photo of Gary standing outside of the restaurant, dark skies, rain coming down, Gary's hood up, with the drawstring cinched so I can barely see the disgusted look on his face.

It's a steady, plodding rain as determined to come down as we are to make progress toward our goal. We're not giving in and neither is the rain.

In contrast, the dark, powerful thunderstorms create torrential downpours that make the clouds give up their moisture in one big burst. The force is intense and short lived. Often, as if spent and defeated the clouds move on, in deference to the sun. The aftermath is quickly dispensed with, and everything is dry and crisp again.

Today, the clouds develop a zen-like existence, merging with the landscape, slowly exhaling the rain in a steady and consistent manner. I feel it on my face and hands, it fills my lungs and creeps up the arms of my jacket. It permeates everything.

My hood is up, I am staring at a space 6 feet in front of my wheel as a blur of asphalt rushes by. I'm in a trance, thoughts float in and out without effort. Hours seem to pass.

"Eric!" Gary yells out and motions me to a shelter at a roadside picnic area.

We're water logged and lethargic. Drooping, saturated rain jackets are peeled off and laid over a bench. Small puddles form underneath them. Mark mumbles in a forsaken manner, "Living the dream." I think to myself, Yup, we're living the hell out of it.

Beside the state map, we have no information about campgrounds other than ones at state parks. Since the Wisconsin map I have came from an atlas, it's too small to even contain information like that. Ashland is about 60 miles from where we started and when we get there we should be able to get advice about local campgrounds.

After a short break, rain jackets that are saturated and glossy on the outside and damp and clammy inside, are put back on. Unenthusiastically we straddle the bikes then push off into the rain.

We trudge along until early evening when we come into Ashland. Gary, who is riding out front, spots a motel and makes a beeline to the door. He goes inside and whips out his credit card before the clerk can greet him. Mark and I can't blame Gary, all of us are really tired of being cold and wet and it's still raining. Besides, we don't know if there are any campgrounds in the area, and even if there are, it wouldn't be much fun setting up while trying to keep all of our gear from getting wet.

It's funny how a little bit of luxury lifted our spirits. We turn up the heat as the fan pumps a warm breeze into the room and takes the cool damp out of the air. We make short use of the pool and hot tub, then back in the room I stand in the shower, hot water wrapped around me like a warm blanket. There is a diner next door and with just fleece jackets on we try to dodge raindrops as we sprint inside. After a good meal and now warm and dry, we prop ourselves up on soft beds to watch cable TV, while laughing and joking.

We are heading southeast today and will be connecting with one of the other touring routes about 40 miles down the road. It's a lazy morning and we take our time eating, then packing up. As we roll our bikes from the room out into the parking lot, the sun shines weakly under partly cloudy skies. The two-lane highway we're on is busy, especially in the city, but the shoulders are wide and we ride without having to battle traffic.

It's another day of short powerful storms followed by bursts of sun. The dark ominous clouds move in with amazing speed. Thunder and lightening ensue then a hard rain falls for a few minutes to a half an hour. Slowly it tapers off then abruptly stops. Shortly after, the sun is out.

We are in the midst of such a storm and I'm riding about 30 feet back of Gary when I see him slow down, then stop. I slowly ride up, "Okay?"

"Yeah, good," Gary says as he twists his torso around to look at me. I coast forward and Gary hops off his bike, leans over his front pannier to shield it from the rain and pulls off the cover to get something out. While it's still raining hard, the clouds break and the sun pushes through turning each raindrop into a burst of light as it hits the road. I look back at Gary as he zips up his pannier, then I stop, grab my camera and take a picture. Mark glides by and I snap a picture of him and Gary too, as he passes. A minute later we're riding under bright sunlight and the rain stops. The glossy road acts like a mirror and I can see the reflection of Mark and Gary in it until the bulk of the water flows off the to the side and the pavement starts to dry.

In the early afternoon we hit Glidden, Wisconsin, and pick up the

North Lakes route, which we're following to Mackinaw City, where Michigan's upper and lower peninsulas connect. That route starts in Minneapolis and heads northeast for the first part until it reaches this point, then heads in a mostly eastern direction.

We stay on Highway 13 until we reach Butternut where we stop for a late lunch. Afterward we are directed down a less traveled and more scenic county highway but encounter many hills, some long with steep grades. By the time we make it to Mercer it's early evening and we've covered 84 miles. With the rain and hills it's been a tiring day. We find a place to eat and a campground just outside of town.

As I come out of a deep sleep I notice the sun is shining and am thankful we don't have to break camp in the rain. We ride into town for breakfast and the sun stays out, but is blocked by a layer of clouds soon after. The rain starts around mid morning and isn't hard enough to predict it will soon pass, but heavier than an all day rain. If a brief thunderstorm comes down in a fury and is over in 10 minutes, I think this hard rain might last an hour or so based on the seemingly logical but rather unscientific idea that a cloud can hold only a certain amount of water.

Our route is pleasant, the road winds through thick forest over a well-maintained road with mild, gently rolling hills and no wind to speak of. And as the hours pass the rain doesn't let up. So much for logic.

In the first half of this segment we saw more rain than in any other, not only in hours but intensity too. Sometimes it would rain for a long time at a steady rate, sometimes it rained hard for a short period of time or would drizzle all day as if riding in a fog. As the week progressed, we all joked that as soon as Gary leaves the tour, the weather will improve. Once, in jest, Mark said, "Gary, why don't you call your wife and have her pick you up right now because we're pretty sick and tired of being wet all the time."

Just past noon we stop for a break and ride off the pavement to a spot under a big tree with broad leaves. It cuts the intensity of the rain but doesn't shut it out completely. We stand there straddling our bikes fed up with being cold and clammy. When we did get a chance to dry out it never lasted very long. We keep trying to laugh it off but we had run out of ways to talk about it without sounding repetitive and cliché.

A little while later we ride up to a coffee house in Boulder Junction and take advantage of the opportunity to dry out a bit and get a warm drink. I order a large double mocha and Gary grabs some biscotti for all of us. It feels good to be in a warm, dry place but we're all damp, the moisture has soaked through to our skin. I take my rain pants off and droop them over the back of my chair along with my jacket. It's warm inside but I can't seem to shake the chill. I place both of my hands around the hot cup of my thick, chocolaty drink.

Our usual heavy, hearty laughs were more like smiles and nods as we force small talk in order to avoid leaving the dry warmth for the dank cold. The rain outlasts us. When we could procrastinate no longer, I put on my pants and don the damp jacket. I step out the door and stand under the eave then flip up my hood and put my helmet on over it. As I walk to the bike I can hear the large raindrops smack the helmet and feel them on the top of my shoulders. We continue down the road toward Conover.

The rain pelts my face and hands and gives the road a three dimensional shimmer on top of its dark and glossy surface. I fall into a steady rhythm and am not focused on anything, just looking ahead.

My mind wanders as we ride single file, 20 yards or more apart. With all the rain we're getting I'm surprised that none has seeped into any of the plastic containers I'm using. The box on the rear of the bike and the small one on the handlebars have plastic lids that snap shut. There is overlap in the design of the lids but with the blowing rain I didn't know if there might be a little water that would dribble in. I can find no evidence that even a drop had penetrated either container. My front panniers are wastebaskets covered by waterproof fabric with a drawstring around the edge to cinch it down. The lip around the wastebaskets prevents the cover from falling off or blowing away once the drawstring is pulled tight, and I didn't see any moisture seep inside these either.

The rear panniers are another story. They're made of waterproof fabric but have many seams where water can leak in. You're supposed to seal the seams with a transparent, caulk-like goo and use rain covers that protect all but the back side where they attach to the bike. In spite of doing this, there were times when the contents got wet.

When I first bought my panniers I didn't find any plastic containers specifically made to haul gear on bicycles, but that doesn't mean they didn't exist. It's possible they look too odd to catch on, or stores didn't want to carry them. But I'd also be surprised if others didn't have the same idea and built their own homemade solution.

Later in the afternoon the rain finally stops and it clears to the point where we almost see some sun, but then it starts to rain again. Although we had some long days, in fact, yesterday we biked 85 miles, most of the time when it rains we come up short of our average. On this segment, short, intense rain showers didn't seem to slow us down much, but all day rain definitely impeded our progress.

We stop for dinner in Conover and with just 57 miles covered since breakfast, we are ready to call it a night. After dinner we find a place to camp. Thankfully it stops raining long enough to set up the tents but never completely clears and looks like it might come down again as we retire.

Up to Gary's last day of riding with us, it had rained every day at some point. Today is no exception. I wake to a hard rain and am waiting for a break to pack up. When the tapping of large drops trails off to a light patter, I scamper to the rest room but the downpour quickly resumes. Walking out the door I find Mark standing under the eave watching small ponds form in the open area where our tents are pitched, saggy and listing. The road into the campground tilts slightly and has a gentle downward slope, which has formed an impressive little river. We stand in silence for a while staring at large raindrops pelt our saturated tents, then Mark says, "Besides another wet ride we're going to be packing up 5 pounds of water."

I let out a sigh and then with a smile on my face, enthusiastically say, "We're living the dream, baby, living the dream!" and we laugh.

It's a bit easier to laugh now, before we start riding and are cold and wet. Besides, there's really no use in complaining. No matter what the weather or any other condition, unless we're physically incapacitated we'll get on the bikes and make some progress toward our goal. In such situations, we all believed things would eventually get better.

The rain lets up a bit and we scramble into our tents to pack and don raingear, but the ferocious storm kicks up again. After sitting there for five minutes and realizing there isn't going to be a good time to break camp, I unzip the tent door, load my gear and start to collapse the tent.

Gary had left and Mark is engaged in the same frantic exercise. We bike up to the building where we had registered and find Gary sitting on a bench on the covered porch. Again, we wait for a few minutes to see if the rain will let up a little and when it does, we take off.

This afternoon we'll meet up with Gary's wife, Gail, and their young daughter, Emma. The destination hasn't been decided on yet. Gail is driving up from the Detroit area and we'll continue along the route, most likely crossing into Michigan before we see her.

After a few hours of riding, the rain lets up but the clouds refuse to move on and we ride under a gray sky. We continue to make our way toward the border along Highway A and just after noon we come through the small town of Nelma and cross the state line into Michigan.

An hour and a half later we are at an ice cream shop waiting for Gary's wife to pick him up. Gary asks Mark and I what kind of ice cream we're eating in a manner that implies it was us, not him, who couldn't ride by without stopping. The video camera is rolling.

"Amaretto cherry, Mackinaw Island fudge," I say.

"Cinnamon pecan twirl," Mark says, then quickly adds, "And I just want to thank you, Gary, for picking this fine establishment." We all laugh.

We are just inside the Michigan border, amid a small megalopolis that includes Mineral Hills, Iron River, Stambaugh, Caspian, and Gaastra for a total population of just under 5000.

Considering how this segment has gone so far, Mark and I are wondering if Gary isn't doing the smart thing. Of course, we're never going to let him live down the fact that his wife is bailing him out. Well, that's our interpretation of what's happening and he isn't going to finish the tour, so neither of us are willing to give up our gloating rights just yet. But if the rain keeps up it's going to be a tough and miserable week.

It isn't long before Gail pulls into the parking lot. Gary is excited to see his wife and their daughter, and after loading his bike and gear, we hang out for a while before saying goodbye. Being the good sport that he is, Gary rolls the video camera and lets Mark and I have the last word, knowing full well that we are going to give him a hard time about leaving the tour. Mark and I ramble on for a few minutes as we all laugh and then Gary jumps in the van and we wave as they drive down the road.

Mark turns toward me, "I asked the guy inside if there was a place in town to do laundry and he said there's one just up the street here."

"Sounds good." We ride off toward the Laundromat.

Just like on the plains, when Gary couldn't come with us, it's a different ride without him and now, shortly after they drove off, I can feel it. Gary's frequent laughter and excessive taunting is a good balance with Mark's more contemplative, quiet demeanor.

As washing machines fill with water, I'm thinking about the trip. A great adventure is determined not solely by its destination nor is it defined exclusively by the things that go right, but also by the challenges faced and overcome. This trip, from coast to coast certainly qualifies. From the harsh learning curve at the start of the trip, to the incessant climbing through the mountains, to the battles with the wind on the plains, and the never-ending rain that resulted in a constant state of cool and soggy. And these things were endured on top of physical aliments, mechanical malfunctions and minor arguments and miscommunications.

Yet nothing dampened our spirits or lessened the joy of our camaraderie, the exhilaration of downhill runs at breakneck speed, the sense of accomplishment at standing next to the Welcome To... sign at the edge of the road on the border of the next state, the ferocious wind deliriously pushing us along a gently rolling, unobstructed landscape, the contemplative still and quiet of the forest at sun set, rhythmically floating in the saddle without sense of the time, day or date, or any other number of soul enriching experiences. Nor could any challenge prevent the laughter; from the constant taunting and poking fun at each other to the way we could see the ridiculousness of unusual or difficult situations. Yeah, it's been a good trip.

We had been riding for 9 days now and have about another week to go. While I'm anxious to complete the journey, mostly I'm resigned that it will be over soon.

When finished with laundry, we get back on State Road 424, a paved back road carved through the forest. There are some long, steep hills with tough climbs, but it hadn't rained since late morning and it's warm but not hot, so we're thankful for the good things as our pace slows and we press hard on the pedals.

We arrive in Crystal Falls in the early evening and ride through town and down a hill to reach the campground. Just as we are setting up our wet, soggy tents it starts to rain again. It's a light rain and we decide to wait and see if it stops before heading to dinner. We sit on a picnic table under a large tree and it rains for maybe half an hour, then we jump back on our bikes and without the burden of gear, zoom up the hill and find a place to eat. By the time we come back the sun is shining and the sky had cleared. The tents have dried out a bit, to the point they aren't sopping wet, and it's a pleasant evening. We take the nice weather in stride without looking ahead. There is a good chance it'll be cloudy and raining by sunrise.

True to our joking predictions, the next day we wake to sunny skies and not a cloud in sight. We couldn't really blame Gary, but it's funny that the day after he leaves the tour, the weather changes. I look up at the sky through the trees and I'm astonished. I turned toward Mark, "Can you believe it?" Mark shakes his head no, as we both laugh. Delighted with the opportunity to dry out our tents, we bike back up the hill for breakfast before breaking camp.

On the way back we are riding around big puddles on a gravel road when a car comes up behind us. I move to the side and see that I won't be able to avoid a puddle that's about 3 feet across. I slow down but when my tire crossed the edge it drops down 10 inches. The tire hits the bottom and bounces up, the lid on my handlebar box pops open and my camera springs to the top. For what is a fraction of a second, but seems much longer, the camera balances on the edge of the box much like a basketball spinning on the rim of the last shot of a championship game, before falling to the side and on the ground. In that brief moment I feel surprise replaced by anticipation, helplessness and finally panic. I immediately stop and reach down for the camera. A piece on the side had broken off and the back was open, but only a little, exposing the film and ruining a few frames. The lens is fine and the camera seems to work. I fire off a few shots at the ground to advance the film past the part that was exposed. I'm relieved the camera wasn't broken but mad about the unusual circumstances that combined to create this situation. I use my shirt to wipe off the wet dirt as if that's a way of fixing the damage and easing my disappointment. I sigh, then pull the rear half of my bike out of the puddle. I examine the Velcro latch, trying to determine how it had failed and figure the force of the drop into the puddle was enough to tear it loose. I put the camera in the box, snap the lid shut, reattach the Velcro and ride back to camp.

I tell Mark what happened. "Does it still work?"

"Yeah, I lost a few pictures but I think the rest will be fine."

We finish breaking camp. The tent is light and fluffy as I grab it with two hands, yank it into the air and shake it. This is a far cry from the heavy and wet blob I'm used to packing. I had placed my rain gear in the sun before we ate and it's also dry. I carefully fold it and put it away.

We take off with our sights set on Escanaba, which is on the northern shore of Lake Michigan. It will be a relatively long day but if the weather stays nice we shouldn't have a problem making it.

It's warm, bordering on hot, as we zip along without jackets on, a rare occurrence so far on this segment. The sun-baked pine trees release a scent that saturates the air like incense. The reddish brown bark of the Red Pines compliments the many shades of green from pine needles to broad-leafed trees to brush and ground cover. The pavement is bone dry and we're energized as we glide along. I look up a few times throughout the morning and don't see a single cloud. The vast, light blue sky is a welcome change. Still, I can't help but think, with the speed at which thunderstorms move in, it wouldn't be surprising if the weather dramatically changed before the day is through. But so far it's gorgeous.

We pass just a few small towns and in early afternoon stop in Hardwood at a convenience store to purchase some cold drinks, one to consume on the spot and one to pack away for further down the road. It's hot but not unpleasant and we're making good progress toward our day's goal.

Early in the evening, a few miles after the town of Schaffer, we turn directly east and confront a mild headwind that slows us down. We are committed to finish the day in Escanaba, which is only about 10 miles away, but I feel I'm running out of energy. At our next break I look at the map and realize we'll top 80 miles before we hit the campground. If there was a place to eat, we could stop for dinner and that would be enough of a break to make the rest of the mileage seem inconsequential. But there is nothing before we reach the city so we dig in and push forward.

When we reach Escanaba we quickly find a restaurant and it feels good to sit in a soft chair, have a cold drink and a hot meal. The campground is just out of town and we dawdled down the road to get a campsite. Tents go up, gear is unloaded, sleeping bags are fluffed. After a shower, I'm walking back to the campsite and notice the sky is still cloudless. The air cools and I put on my fleece jacket. The sun is close to the horizon and filters through the densely wooded area. In the last moments of twilight I sit at the picnic table on our site and think back to the morning. Not a speck of rain fell all day. I open my journal to record the highlights and notice it is Sunday. Yes indeed, truly a Sun Day.

I wake to the sound of rain. As I lay there I let out a loud sigh, discouraged at the thought of trudging along, hands and feet cold and wet, the rest of my body damp and clammy, like so many other days. A few moments later I sit up and unzip my tent window. I can see Mark's tent, it's about 15 feet away. I shout over, "Living the dream, buddy!" I can hear Mark laughing. "I'm glad it's raining again because one day of sunshine is about all I can take."

"At least we don't have to worry about getting sunburn."

"Yeah, because that would be a real tragedy."

The Elite can always see that the glass is half full, as long as it comes with a liberal dose of sarcasm and laughter.

The rain tapers off, then stops and we break camp but it starts up again as we approach the restaurant. We stop at a place that's divided into many small rooms much like an old Victorian house. In a front room at a small table just big enough for two, we sit among a handful of other patrons. The waitress hands us menus.

Bacon seems like such a decadent food. Fatty, greasy, heavy on the preservatives, hormone induced, but such a great flavor. I generally resist it knowing that it can't possibly be good for me but it's raining, the 10th day out of 11 and I'm ready for some decadence.

"What'll ya have?"

"Bacon, crisp. Eggs, over easy. Hash browns with lots of butter and well done. And, um, wheat toast." Hey, I got to have something healthy.

There is a big window that looks out to the street. From where I sit I can see it's coming down steady throughout breakfast and it's not going to let up. As we finish our coffee, Mark looks at me and says, "Ready?"

I'm full and content. I look over, through the window to the rain. "Yes, I believe I am."

As we bundle up, jump on the bikes and pedal down the road, I refuse to imagine that our good-weather luck had run out. Now that we are back in our home state I'm a little more familiar with the climate and know we are due for a change. It's the end of June and the rainy spring weather should be over. Besides, in 11 days of riding we had just one when it didn't rain, so the odds are in our favor.

We head north along the coast of Little Bay De Noc until we are able to skirt around the northern most point and head east. We're on Highway 2, which is the main road along the southern part of the U.P. so traffic is heavier as we trudge along in the rain. Around noon it stops but the clouds block out the sun and hang low in the sky. Pavement dries from wet and glossy, to damp. The raingear comes off at the next break.

It's a warm but dull gray day and Mark and I ride in silence for a long time. I keep thinking about the end of the trip. In miles, we are quite a ways from the end, but in days it's only a week, barring some unusual situation.

At times it seems like it's been a much longer trip because we stretched it out over a period of 4 years. Between segments we would make plans for the upcoming one and talk about new gear or lessons learned. We would also recount funny stories and seemingly laugh as hard as when things happened, even through numerous retellings.

While many were astonished at our plans, both at home and along the route, I never doubted our resolve or ability to finish, mainly because I didn't see the trip as a challenge that was beyond our capabilities. Following a map or riding a bike are common, simple things that don't require much intellect. Physically, powering a bike is something any reasonably fit person can do. Making a commitment of time isn't easy, and facing day-to-day challenges can tax even the hardiest soul, but are not impossible. Yet, it wasn't any thing individually but the combination of all these things that made this a challenge. And to many who weren't doing the trip, something that seemed exceedingly difficult. Now, looking at the trip not in reference to the immediate challenge, the issues we were facing on any given day, but overall, it's easier to see the magnitude of it.

I think about riding into Mark's driveway on the last day of the trip and feel a serene sense of accomplishment, followed by slight melancholy that this experience will soon be over. This feeling seems to fight the anxiousness of rushing to the end the closer we get to it. And now, the 12th day in without a break, I feel a little road weary, especially after all the rain we've had.

We ride into Manistique in the early evening and find a place to eat. After, the nearby campground has a motel up front, with wooded sites in the back and we have access to the indoor pool and sauna. We set up, then splash around for a while and when we walk back to the tents at twilight it's lightly raining again.

It's a cool morning, buried in the woods among tall trees and overgrown scrub but the sun is piercing the thick canopy with spotlights of warm, bright light. Gear is packed and loaded, then we make our way out of the cover of the forest and back toward the road. There is a restaurant in town, and soon we're back on Highway 2. In spite of the sunshine and nearly cloudless sky the air is cool enough for a jacket.

Early in the day there are some brief views of Lake Michigan but the highway turns inland and we are riding among tall trees and dense forest. At Gulliver we head north and a nice wind pushes us along. This same wind makes riding difficult when we turn east near Blaney Park. The temperature warms up, I peel my jacket off and it feels like the perfect biking weather. The crosswind thwarts our forward progress but seems to dissipate as the road and coast merge. We are now riding close to the shore with sweeping views of Lake Michigan. Wide sandy beaches reach out and under shimmering blue water. Clusters of trees occasionally break the long stretch of sandy shore into separate beaches but the undeveloped coast seems endless. The sun is on us full blast but the air is mild with a light breeze coming off the lake and it seems as if it couldn't be a more perfect combination.

Mid afternoon, we pull off the road and walk out in the sand toward the lake. It's quiet except for the sound of waves hitting the sand and seagulls in the air. We just sit there silently enjoying the solitude and the 180 degree panorama of lake stretching out to meet the sky at the horizon. I lean back propping myself up with my elbows. With eyes gazing toward the lake I say, "Sure am glad we got rid of Gary." We laugh.

Such a nice day dulled the memory of all those times we were wet and soggy, and we're reveling in every minute of it. "Living the dream," Mark says after an extended silence. "Oh yeah," I reply laying in the sun, the breeze gently caressing my skin.

We had covered 77 miles when we stopped for dinner near Brevot. I'm tired, ready to camp and there are a few campgrounds nearby. We eat in a small restaurant that's inhabited by just a few other patrons. I order lasagna, one of my favorites, and it's excellent. We're in no hurry to leave and I have a nice, stout cup of coffee and chocolate torte for dessert. We linger in the dining room for a while then walk outside toward the lake, taking in the view.

Back at the bikes we both unfold our maps and look over the location of the campgrounds. Mark is looking further down the road and suggests we ride to the straits. His argument is bolstered with the idea of taking the ferry to Mackinac Island tomorrow morning and spending a good part of the day there. This is appealing because I wanted to spend some time on the Island and I could use a break from biking all day, or perhaps the feeling of needing to get to the next destination. The campground at the straits is another 20 miles down the road. I would have rejected this idea before we ate, but now I feel rested, the sun is out, we have plenty of time before dark, it's warm and the riding had been superb. We take off for the straits.

We're still on Highway 2, which is the same road the three of us had been on, for the most part, since Washington. We take it to the end, the Mackinac Bridge that connects Michigan's upper and lower peninsulas, which is where we'll also leave the touring route and head down the western shore of Lake Huron.

The campground is in a state park that's at the tip of the point next to the bridge. Gear is unloaded, tents are set up and showers taken. We walk to a clearing that has a good vantage point for viewing the bridge. As we take some photos and walk around, I happen to look down and notice a 20 dollar bill at my feet. I pick it up and ask Mark if he dropped some money. He looks at the small fanny pack that he keeps his valuables in and it's zipped tight. "Nope." There are some people in the area but none of them are close by or appear to be looking for something. "Guess it's my lucky day." Then I hold up the bill and say, "Know what we should do with this?"

A few minutes later we're licking large ice cream cones while walking back to the campsite. "Good idea," Mark says through a mouthful of Butter Pecan.

"Living the dream," I respond through a mouthful of Chocolate, Chocolate Chip.

Mark and I get up early and head to the ferry station. We plan on spending most of the day on Mackinaw Island, then take the other ferry to the Lower Peninsula to find a place to camp. The Island is small, about two miles wide by three miles long but it boasts the famous Victorian-style Grand Hotel with the world's longest porch, excellent fudge, historical sites and is one of the few places in this country where automobiles are prohibited.

It's a short two-block ride to the terminal. We buy our tickets, walk the bikes aboard and 10 minutes and approximately five miles later we're there. We make a loop of the island on the road that parallels the shore then head inland along some of the trails. We stop and take photos of Arch Rock and ride along narrow paths through the heart of the island with no particular agenda, stopping at various attractions.

After lying on the grass and snacking on dried fruit and candy we take a tour of Mackinaw Fort, which dates to 1780, and other historical landmarks.

We walk along the main business district where there are plenty of opportunities to get some fudge and once we decide on the flavor and quantity we make our way to the terminal.

During the entire trip this is the only time in which we planned on spending most of the day not riding toward our destination. It was a welcome break and if it were up to me there would have been more.

With plenty of daylight to spare, we board the 5:00 ferry to the Lower Peninsula. We disembark in Mackinac City and find a place for dinner. The state maps that are guiding us now only show campgrounds at state parks and we agree to head to Cheboygan State Park about 20 miles away. After dinner we start down highway 23, the road that parallels the western shore of Lake Huron. After a day on the Island, the ride seems anti-climatic and we're ready to camp. We pass a number of roads and houses but don't ride through any towns until we hit Cheboygan. The park and campground are just the other side of the city.

As we're checking in, the ranger notices our bikes and asks about the trip. We talk about heading back to the Detroit area and how it's the end of a cross-country journey. "Do you guys know that at every state campground, if you are on a bicycle, they can't turn you away?" she says.

"Really?" I had never heard of anything like this.

"They have to find you a spot."

"That's good to know."

"I mention it because as we get close to the Fourth of July it's going to be hard to find an available campsite in many places, especially if you're rolling in after 5:00."

I had lost track of time and most days didn't know if it was a Saturday or a Wednesday, let alone the date. I had forgot about the holiday.

"Thanks," I say as we leave.

"Have a good trip."

Our campsite is in a secluded, heavily wooded area that makes it seem like we're the only ones in the park. Big trees shade our site, and brush and small trees provide privacy. The tent is light and dry and I think about cutting the tarp off the top. At some point I tied it to the fly with some cord so I could put both of them on at the same time. I stop and think I might be tempting fate, then realize I am still going to carry the tarp so I might as well use it. I feel good after a leisurely day on the Island and later we sit at the picnic table, Mark writing post cards and I taking notes about the trip.

The next morning I sit up and look out the window of my tent to see rabbits, barely four feet away. For some reason it's always a delight to see wild animals so close, that is, if they're not chewing a hole in your gear, getting ready to attack you, or eating your food. I'm sure they heard me moving around but are content to sit there for awhile as long as I don't make a sudden move or loud noise. Eventually they scamper off and into the woods.

It seems like every morning a weather check is the first thing on my mind as soon as I open my eyes. After two nice, sunny days it's as if we are finally getting the weather we expected and with the sun shining again, suddenly it's an afterthought.

Looking at my crude state map, I can't see a town for at least 25 miles down the road. Not knowing how far we'll have to ride before we come across a restaurant, Mark and I backtrack to Cheboygan for a hot meal. Including the distance we rode into the park to our camp-site, the trip to the restaurant and back meant that we put 10 miles on our bikes before we made any forward progress. As we ride back I figure this is another thing that would seem ridiculous to bikers interested in covering the most miles in the least amount of time, but it sounded better to us than gnawing on granola bars until we came across a place to eat. Besides, being part of The Elite often means that serious biking takes a backseat to things like goofing off, laughing and joking, stopping for a hot meal or a sweet treat, or other impor-tant things.

From what we can make out on our maps, Highway 23 runs close to the shore, so it should offer some good views of the lake. We imagine the scenery will match the gorgeous views we had of Lake Michigan along Route 2. Unfortunately it didn't. Throughout the morning there were some nice, brief views of Lake Huron but not to the extent of what we experienced in the U.P.

It's cool today and I'm riding with my wind shell on, which is pref-erable to scorching heat. The partly cloudy sky occasionally blocks the sun, but It doesn't look like we're going to get rained on and we're thankful for that. We continue to ride in a fairly remote area. There are numerous roads that branch off of our route, and houses that break up the huge expanse of forest, but nothing else.

Unfortunately traffic picks up and the condition of the road var-ies. At times the shoulder narrows and it's distressing as cars zip by at freeway speeds. I can imagine many drivers see this as no man's land, a large stretch of forest without services, and are anxious to get to their destination as fast as possible. But it makes it hard for us to enjoy the ride as cars frequently rush by in both directions.

A stop in Rodgers City for lunch gives a much needed break from the conditions of the road. We take our time, hoping the traffic is some kind of anomaly and will ease up.

After lunch I notice the road curves inland. There isn't a chance we'll see Lake Huron before Alpena but the map doesn't offer much of an alternate route if we want to try another road besides 23. We stick with our plan and curve along Grand Lake and then Long Lake as the day wears on. I'm surprised at how heavy the traffic is considering how far north we are. The constant buzz of one car after another rushing by is tiring and it doesn't let up. Again, the shoulders narrow in places and with traffic passing in both directions there isn't much leeway cars can give us. The thought of being hit by a car because of a minor, split second mistake creates moments of high anxiety.

By the time we reach Alpena we had covered almost 90 miles. It had been a tiring day on many accounts. We find a place to eat and somewhere to camp. After we settle in, Mark and I spread the map out and start calculating distances. There are two state parks along our route, one at Tawas City and the other just north of Bay City. That means riding 65 miles or so, for each of the next two days, which is reasonable. From there, it will be a long ride to Mark's on the last day, around 90 miles, maybe a little more. We'll stay on 23 along the coast until Bay City, then follow a direct route to Mark's, east of Pontiac in the northern suburbs of Detroit.

Again, I feel an anxiousness to zip home especially since the riding has not been very pleasant today, but also conflicted with the need to savor the last few days of the trip.

It's a cloudy morning and after breakfast it begins to sprinkle. We put on the rain gear expecting the rain to intensify but 10 minutes later it stops, barely wetting the pavement. We're back on 23 heading south and come to a sign marking the 45th parallel, the point halfway between the North Pole and Equator and stop to take a picture. Even at this early hour traffic seems substantial. It's Friday, and the Fourth of July is Tuesday, so we figured traffic would probably be heavy this weekend.

Every now and again we catch a glimpse of Lake Huron but it's in short slices. The road must be either a little too far inland or the tree and brush cover just too dense. But I'm also surprised to see such a large part of the coast occupied by private or commercial development that blocks the view and prevents access.

Traffic picks up considerably throughout the day and it seems like there is a car racing by every two seconds or less. The crescendo of buzz, slowly building from behind, then peaking as a flash of colored metal appears and a burst of air pushes you to the side, is disturbing enough. We had been experiencing this most of yesterday. Now that it is happening every two seconds, it's maddening.

We stop for a break as cars continue to bolt by individually, or in small groups all following each other closely.

"I don't know about you, but this traffic is really bothersome." I say as we stand in the tall grass just off the shoulder and away from the road.

"I agree, it's annoying."

"I don't know if it's the contrast to all those back roads we took where 15 minutes or more might pass between cars, but this hasn't been pleasant."

"Yeah. I'm sure a lot of this is traffic for the Fourth, and at a different time of the year it wouldn't be so bad." I nod in agreement.

I dig through a pocket on my pannier. "Cinnamon Pop Tart?"

"Sure."

I pull one out of the two-pack and hand Mark the other in the wrapper.

"I did think it would be more scenic, that we'd see the lake a lot more. It looks that way on the map."

"Yeah, I'm surprised by that myself," Mark says as he set his water bottle back in its cage. "Well, at least we have good weather."

"Thank you, Gary." We both laugh.

With a little effort spent on route finding, it is entirely possible we could have found some less traveled roads that were more scenic, but we were hoping that at some point the coastline would open up, traffic would die down and we would experience something similar to the ride along Lake Michigan. At this point it didn't seem very promising. I keep thinking that traffic will be concentrated around the towns we pass and once we're away from them it will be better. Yet, that didn't seem to be true at all.

Later, when we stop for a break again, there is almost a full minute of silence as traffic momentarily vanishes. Unfortunately the parade of cars quickly resumes. "Oh, that was nice."

"Yeah, we just need a couple of days like that."

We ride into Tawas State Park and find the building to register for a campsite. There is a sign outside that says the campground is full. We park the bikes, I walk inside and am greeted by a ranger standing on the other side of the counter.

"Hi, we're looking for a place to camp," I say motioning to Mark and the bikes outside.

"You guys on bikes?"

"Yes."

"Well, the campground is full but I can let you stay in the day use area tonight." He grabbed a paper map of the park off of a stack on the counter. "Here's where we're at, and this is the day use area," he says as he marks up the map. "You can camp anywhere in here, on this side of the road. Not on the beach. And it's the same price as a tent site would be."

"Sounds great. Thanks."

There is brush and tall grass behind us, and across the road a wide panorama of beach and lake. The park is on a peninsula that juts out into Lake Huron and seems isolated from the mainland. We have a great view and there is nobody in sight. After the constant buzz of traffic all day, the quiet, peaceful evening seems that much more serene. A light breeze floats through our campsite and seagulls can be heard in the distance. As the sun touches the horizon, thin wispy clouds turn pink.

We seem to have broken the spell of perpetual rain for good since we've had four days in which it's been mostly sunny with just a sprinkle of rain, and it now looks like today is going to be nice too. It's a great morning, sunny, clear and warm. Our site is tranquil and calm. From overhead, the clear blue sky curves downward into the lake and there is a mild breeze coming in from the horizon. Seagulls glide over the beach and the muffled sound of waves hitting the sand is barely audible. We take our time breaking camp and enjoy the nice morning.

It's a short ride back to highway after breakfast in Tawas. Not far down the road, we come around a curve and see something unusual that makes both of us stare while we try to comprehend what we are seeing and why it is there. Just off the road is a group of adult-size, cartoon characters that look like they are cast in fiberglass or concrete. A four foot tall Winnie the Pooh stands hand in hand with a five foot tall Tigger. Bugs Bunny, Goofy, Mickey Mouse and others stand or sit with happy grins as if waiting for company. Snoopy has Woodstock on his lap and there is a life size Native American on a horse. A small sign welcomes visitors to stop and take pictures. We both laugh and pull off the road as we walk around eyeing these creations. I take out my camera and tripod and set up some photos of Mark and I next to Mickey Mouse and some of the other characters. It seems like such a silly, tourist thing to do, but we can't help ourselves. After a few tough days of riding, it feels good to be frivolous.

The wind is coming from the south and once on the road it's pushing against us. We fight this mild headwind while enduring the urgent rush of heavy traffic throughout the morning. The congestion causes us to ride single file and the buzz of the traffic is too much for conversation. We trudge along hoping for better conditions down the road.

The highway slowly curves 90 degrees and for a while we're heading directly west. The wind shifts as we get deeper into Saginaw Bay, the place between the thumb and fingers on the mitten state. As we curve back, heading south again, we are now fighting a strong crosswind.

We leave 23 behind as it heads west and merges with Interstate 75. We follow a series of streets too small to be drawn on our state map as we continue to head south along the eastern edge of Saginaw Bay. We're too far inland to see the coast but the buildings and trees have helped block the wind so we resist the urge to find a more scenic route. For the next hour and a half or so, traffic is lighter and cars dash by at a slower speed, and that's a relief.

Early in the evening we find a place to eat just outside of Bay City State Recreation Area, our planned destination. After dinner it's a short ride to the park. As we approach the building to register for a campsite, again there is a sign that says the campground is full. We both see it and Mark says, "Go work your magic," as we park the bikes.

I walk inside and approach the counter. "We're on bicycles and looking for a campsite," I say motioning to Mark and the bikes outside.

A young man in uniform on the other side of the counter says, "Sorry, we're full."

"We're on bikes."

"Yeah, we're full. There's a campsite down the road a bit. They might have space."

"I'd like to talk to the Superintendent."

"He's not here."

"Can you call him or just tell me where he's at and I'll go find him."

There was a pause, then he walks to the phone and dials. "Just tell him two guys on bicycles are looking for a campsite."

He stands there looking at me for a few seconds with the phone to his ear then says, "Yeah, it's the front desk. I have two guys on bicycles who want to camp and we're full, but they still want to talk to you." There's a pause, "Yeah." Then he turns away from me and a few seconds later says, "Um, 17." And then, "Okay."

He turns back toward me, hangs up the phone and says, "I can put you in site 17." He grabs a paper map of the park and shows me where the site is, I pay him and we ride off to find the site.

"He didn't want to give you a site, did he?" Mark says as we ride through the campground.

"I just think he didn't know about the bike thing. It's probably just a summer job for him." I was scanning the small posts with the campsite numbers on them. "I think 17 is over there."

We pull up to a site that is among the other ones, arranged like a city block, they way they usually are. "What I don't get is how the campground was full, then magically it wasn't. I thought we'd be in the day use area again." I hop off my bike. "Not that it matters, this is a nice site."

The sites are well spaced and there are plenty of tall trees in the campground. Sometimes the grass gets trampled to the point where you end up camping on dirt at some of the popular places, but the ground cover is thick and green.

We unpack and set up. "In honor of our last night I think we should engage in a full body immersion in Lake Huron," I say.

Mark laughs. "Sounds good to me."

"We started the trip that way, it's appropriate we end it that way."

"I agree, not that Gary would know anything about that." We both laugh again. We enjoy making fun of Gary since he's not here to defend himself, perhaps a little too much.

We have to walk quite a ways to get to the lake and then further to find water deep enough to plunge into but as soon as we can claim bragging rights and splash around a bit, we get out.

Later, we scrutinize the rough maps we have and worry about having to spend time on multi-laned roads with no shoulders as we try to find the shortest route to Mark's house. Figuring our final destination is about 90 miles away and detours are uncertain, Mark sets his watch so we can be up at the crack of dawn. Well, not quite the crack of dawn, but earlier than we usually rise.

"Eric. Eric."
I'm slowly coming out of a deep sleep and into a pre-wake haze.
"Eric."
"Yup."
I roll over and take a deep breath, blink my eyes repeatedly and try to focus. A moment later I sit up. A few moments after that I start to grab my gear and pack.

As we load our bikes, the campground is dead calm and whisper quiet. We barely make a sound as we glide past other sites and down the road out of the park. We start looking for a restaurant and there are a few options.

After breakfast we head south and make our way into Bay City. It's early on a Sunday morning and everything is still as we search for State Road 15, marked as a scenic road on our map. We'll be on this road for a long time before the route finding becomes a real chore. It's sunny and warm already, an indication that it'll be a hot day.

Traffic is much lighter than the previous few days as we ride in a southeasterly direction. We pass quite a few farms that seem like they're on the small side for a commercial venture, a size that a farmer would have a hard time making a living off of. I imagine the families up early to harvest the ripe crops, boxing them up and heading to local stores or farmer's markets.

Mark seems anxious and sets a moderate pace. Soon he is far ahead. I know it's going to be a long day and feel more comfortable plodding along. Over the next half hour Mark slows and matches my pace. This happens without discussion.

We turn directly south and stay on 15 for hours. As time passes and we get closer to Flint, one of the larger cities in Michigan, traffic picks up considerably. We won't have to ride through the city, but we'll be just east of it and cross Interstate 69 too. Riding conditions are getting tougher. We can see it coming bit by bit and then we're in it. We're fighting traffic, riding on small shoulders, trying to cross busy streets and looking for alternatives to the urban sprawl. We dealt with this in Rochester, New York on the east segment and when we came back from Canada last fall. While there doesn't seem to be an easy solution to fighting congestion when we are off route, it's as if we forgot what a hassle this is and simply didn't put much effort into finding better maps or figuring out a route ahead of time. A day or two under these conditions is tolerable but too much of this, let's-just-wing-it-with-a-state-map idea doesn't cut it. I didn't want to admit it, but the end of the trip would have been more enjoyable if we had planned better.

We take 15 until Ortonville then head in a southeastern direction toward Mark's house. We are still a few hours from our destination and the riding isn't pleasant, the conditions are poor and it's quite hot. When the shoulders are bad we ride on the white line on the side of the road and many motorists don't want to cede an inch as they zoom by. Our map doesn't offer enough detail to provide many options. Roads large enough to be shown on the map are large enough to host heavy traffic.

We arrive in Lake Orion an hour or so later and it feels good to recognize familiar surroundings. We find a place to eat and slump down in the seats, tired not just from the long ride but also the exasperating conditions. At this point we've come almost 90 miles.

A respite comes after dinner when we veer onto the Paint Creek Trail, a popular Rail Trail. For 8.5 miles the packed gravel trail accounts for the nicest riding of the day. The path is wide and smooth and traverses a heavily wooded area along Paint Creek. A bonus in riding the trail in a southerly direction is a mild downhill grade, and we sail along.

Mark and I have been on this trail numerous times, and it's about 6 miles from his house so the rest of the way is familiar. We zigzag through the neighborhood and clock 100 miles when we pull into Mark's driveway, the end of a journey that, all segments included, lasted 63 days and covered over 4,200 miles.

"We made it!" I say as we both stop and hop off our bikes. Mark walks over and sticks out his hand, "Congratulations!" I give it a hearty shake. "And congratulations to you as well." We are grinning like fools and can't stop. My mind is reeling with memories of the trip, trying to comprehend the magnitude of it.

We started with no touring experience and a few wild expectations. It was perseverance, not impeccable planning or superior intelligence that allowed us to quickly adapt and keep moving forward. It was the love of adventure and exploration, not just of the land, but of the unknown and our abilities as well, that made us excited to embrace the next day, the next segment.

Our lives are seemingly made of a long series of moments that range from minor tasks and mundane chores to family events, hanging out with friends and the day-to-day grind of work. These are the things that seem to unfold themselves without effort or planning, the things that are numerous, short lived and become part of our routines. These nondescript moments provide a balance, a backdrop, to the big events and life changing moments that tend to define our past and summarize our lives.

This is one of those big moments, the end result of one of those big events.

www.ingramcontent.com/pod-product-compliance
Lightning Source LLC
Chambersburg PA
CBHW071537040426
42452CB00008B/1046